Rooms to Grow

Creating Rooms and Furniture for Children

by Jane Cornell

CREATIVE HOMEOWNER PRESS®

MW00569598

COPYRIGHT © 1993
CREATIVE HOMEOWNER PRESS®
A Division of Federal Marketing Corp.
Upper Saddle River, NJ

Manufactured in the United States of America

Current Printing (last digit)
10 9 8 7 6 5 4 3 2 1

Rooms to Grow: Creating Rooms and Furniture for Children
Author: Jane Cornell
LC: 92-74444
ISBN: 1-880029-16-2 (paper)

CREATIVE HOMEOWNER PRESS®
A Division of Federal Marketing Corp.
24 Park Way
Upper Saddle River, NJ 07458

Creative Director: Warren Ramezzana
Editor: Kimberly Kerrigone
Graphic Designers: Annie Jeon, Warren Ramezzana
Photo Researchers: Jane Cornell, Kimberly Kerrigone
Illustrators: James Randolph, Norm Nuding,
        Warren Ramezzana
Electronic Production: Annie Jeon, Warren Ramezzana,
        Mindy Circelli, Kimberly Kerrigone

Cover Design: Warren Ramezzana
Cover Photograph: GenCorp

Electronic Prepress: M.E. Aslett Corporation
Printed at: Webcrafters, Inc.

Safety First

Though all the designs and methods in this book have been tested for safety, it is not possible to overstate the importance of using the safest methods possible. What follows are reminders; some do's and don'ts of basic do-it-yourself building techniques. They are not substitutes for your own common sense.

Use caution, care, and good judgment when following the procedures described in this book.

Always wear eye protection.

Wear the appropriate gloves when handling chemicals, heavy construction or when sanding.

Be sure that the electrical setup is safe; be sure that no circuit is overloaded, and that all power tools and electrical outlets are properly grounded. Do not use power tools in wet locations.

Read container labels on paints, solvents and other products; provide ventilation, and observe all warnings.

Be aware that there is never time for your body's reflexes to save you from injury from a power tool; be alert!

Know the limitations of your tools and do not try to force them to do what they were not designed to do.

Do not change a blade or a bit unless the power cord is unplugged.

Use holders or pushers to work pieces shorter than 3" on a table saw or jointer. Whenever possible, cut small pieces from larger pieces.

Do not wear loose clothing, hanging hair, open cuffs, or jewelry while working. Keep your hands away from the business ends of blades, cutters and bits. Hold a portable circular saw with both hands so that you know where your hands are at all times.

Do not support a workpiece with your leg or any other part of your body when sawing or drilling. Clamp small pieces firmly to a work surface.

Do not carry sharp or pointed tools; use a special-purpose tool belt with leather pockets and holders instead.

Flammable or volatile materials such as paints and finishes should only be stored in approved storage containers. Never store flammable liquids near radiators, heating units, fireplaces, chimneys or flues; or near any electrical equipment.

Table of Contents

Introduction

Everyone has experience with childhood, because we all were children once. But beyond this common link, it is all too easy to lose the necessary understanding of the specific needs of a child today. It takes a fresh new look to create a child's environment that defends individual needs and helps prepare a child for the fast-changing society in which he or she will be growing up.

Adults often remember, from their own early years, favorite beds (or bunk fortresses), the delight of furniture just to size, perhaps a magical storage trunk or doll trunk for keeping things in place, treasured (or despised) wallcoverings and paint colors, and a host of special aspects of the rooms they called their own. A number of these will be equally treasured by today's lucky children. However, they will have a host of new acquisitions that were uncommon in their parent's childhood.

Parents today are raising electronic wizards, whose keyboard savvy extends from video games to computerized learning tools. Kids caught up in a computer game or project can spend large amounts of time in front of the screen. Such restricted intensity calls for good seating, the appropriate lighting and the right kind of desk surface.

Intercom systems that connect parents with kids' rooms for sound monitoring were fairly uncommon a decade ago, and are considered indispensable to many new parents today. The needs for sound monitoring and noise control are also more important to parents today who live closer to neighbors, in condos or townhouses, rather than the individual homes in which they grew.

Just as some of the easy-care, wash-and-wear clothes of today are light-years ahead in convenience to those of the past, so are the adjustable, mix-and-matchable furnishings that are designed for kids today.

The challenge, then, in designing children's rooms is to sort through the multitude of choices available, and to hit upon those that best suit you and your child. In broad terms, this book covers the needs at each stage of a child's growing, in his own room and for the home in general. We start with the latest in safety information, including some vital cautions about recycling older products. Just as adult furniture is most successful when it is designed specifically for adult bodies, children's furnishings work best when designed for the special size, shape and capabilities of kids. We'll cover some ergonomic considerations (body relating to its environment) to factor in as a child grows.

There's never been a better time to buy children's furnishings, since many furniture manufacturers are now gearing up to create products just for this age group. And the manufacturers and retailers who have been the mainstays for kid's rooms throughout the years have perfected their products.

Also included in this book are designs for making the heirlooms that can be cherished for generations to come. Some plans, such as the one for the Shaker-style stool, can be easily undertaken by a do-it-yourself beginner. Others, such as an Early American Changing table, may challenge the woodsmith's talent.

It's the total personality that makes a child's room so distinctive. Nursery design comes out of the parent's heads, where they combine practical elements to make a dream room for the anticipated but undefined dream child. In seemingly no time at all that unknown child is a full personality with his own emerging style. Here's a chance to factor in and meld your ideas and hers. . . and who's to say which is more whimsical, which more practical, parent or child!

To help create a room's personality, we have included space and moneysaving ways to use colors and textures, to treat walls, ceilings and windows, to anchor it all with playable flooring and to create an ideal lighting environment. Even heating and ventilation deserve special attention.

Sleeping, feeding and changing are the main activities to be addressed in the newborn's room. As time progresses, special spaces and considerations need to be carved out. Included are exercise areas, play areas, study centers, an incorporation of video/sound systems, and storage, storage, storage!

Shared children's rooms call for special strategies. Whether it's the everyday use of two or more siblings or an occasional overnight guest, a grade school kid's room needs to answer the challenge of room for more than just one. Divide and conquer tactics, along with the furnishings that suit them, can make a room comfortable for a crowd.

While a child's room is specifically devoted to his needs and interests, any parent knows that a child's interests and needs take over practically every square foot of living space and then some. Playrooms can be centers for the entire family, roughhouse spots for kids only, or multiuse spaces that adjust to whatever activity strikes the family's fancy. Kitchens and bathrooms in an active child's home first and foremost must be safely designed. . . and then they can be creatively enhanced to include both large and small family members. Carving out play niches, from basement to attic, may transform a formerly cramped home into a child's heaven without over-running the grown-up space.

Like the old lady who lived in the shoe, any parent can become overwhelmed at the drastic space demands that a child seemingly makes on any home. But armed with checklists and good plans, order will be restored.

Who Lives Here?

In the beginning, the entire family lives in the baby's room or wherever the baby is at the moment. Life centers around the feeding and sleeping of the newest family member. As time progresses, a child's room becomes a place apart from other family spaces. It takes on the parents' wishes for the child and the child's own character. Whether the decorating scheme is to be classic or totally new and unique, the goal will be to create a balanced room that is both soothing and stimulating.

Through the astounding spurts of development and growth of early years, a room must be transformed and updated to keep abreast of the child's needs. While major changes often are not called for, there are some evolutions in furnishing that can make all the difference between a loved space that's conducive to learning and a malfunctioning space that simply does not work. Equally important, your safety considerations for a child must change as a child expands his limits in competence and also danger.

To understand how a room can affect a growing child, start with a rudimentary understanding of each developmental stage, then match this with basic safety considerations, and also weigh in the likely size and space requirements for the child. Kids aren't just little adults, and each age brings with it a new set of needs, all relevant to good room design.

Few basics are necessary for a nursery; many parents opt to keep furnishings simple while adding character with a more elaborate wall treatment. Keep in mind, a coordinated color scheme will help visually control the clutter.

Ages & Stages

Not all children progress at the same rate. Developmental spurts and lags are normal childhood occurrences. However, it is important to anticipate the next stages in planning children's rooms. Often, a long-range plan saves money because you incorporate furnishings that are flexible enough to be useful for years. Equally important, you can put into place the necessary safety precautions before your child is old enough to get himself into danger. The following are some hallmarks of various stages from the Better Sleep Council and the American Academy of Pediatrics.

Infants: The First Year. Newborns can sleep 16 hours a day or longer, but their sleep periods are fairly brief and irregular. As their nervous systems develop, babies become capable of sleeping five or six hours at a time, often by the age of six months (though 10 percent of 1-year-olds have not yet slept for six hours straight). You'll want to have the baby sleep close by, or have your own comfortable area in the nursery for the round-the-clock months. Generally, babies do not need night feedings after their fourth month, although this depends upon development and size.

From birth to 6 months accidents often happen because parents are not aware of what their child can do. In no time at all a child who can barely lift his head will be wiggling off a bed or reaching for your cup of coffee. As soon as a baby's born, she will wiggle and move and push against things with her feet, which can result in a fall. As she grows, she will suddenly be able to roll over and fall off everything, and must never be left unprotected. She may be able to crawl as early as 6 months, calling for gates on stairways and entrances of rooms where she might hurt herself.

At 3 to 5 months babies wave their fists and grab at things. Even at this age, never eat, drink or carry anything hot near your baby or while holding her. She'll be exploring her environment by putting anything and everything into her mouth, so make sure all small objects (including hard pieces of food) are out of reach. If you plan to use a playpen, start putting the baby into it a little each day starting at about 3 months.

At 6 months, infants may cry at night for a number of reasons, including separation anxiety. Sleep experts generally recommend that you wait for a minute before going to the child to provide reassurance, and let the baby learn how to fall asleep alone. This is the beginning of the favorite blanket or stuffed animal substitute to provide nighttime emotional comfort. From 7 to 12 months, an infant will suddenly be able to roll over, crawl, sit and stand. She may climb before she can walk, or walk with support months before you

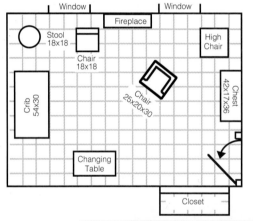

expect. She will be able to grasp at or reach almost anything. Protect her by never leaving hot liquids or food on tables or counter edges, keeping poisonous materials locked up and out of reach, and removing sharp-edged or hard furniture on which she might climb.

Although she's more mobile, an infant's newly formed love of water makes bathing and other water activities dangerous, requiring constant vigilance. If you haven't checked your plants for possible poison potential, do so now and eliminate these dangers.

Toddlers: Ages 1 to 3. This age begins the most accident-prone stage of a child's life, largely because the child will walk, run, climb, jump and explore everything. Since he can now open bottles easily and he will continue to put things in his mouth, all medicines must have safety caps. He'll exalt in opening doors and drawers, getting into and on top of everything, and in taking things apart. Even walking can be unsteady, though climbing, running and jumping have become acquired skills. Lock doors to dangerous areas, make sure windows have window guards and check that you aren't providing tempting climbing objects, such as a chair leading to a window. Keep sharp-edged furniture away from his area.

Coordinated wallcoverings, borders and fabrics make it easy to draw a color scheme together and provide a theme for the room. When children begin to socialize in grade school, rooms often include sleep-over facilities and lots of playspace.

The bathroom and kitchen are both danger areas for this mighty explorer. When parents are distracted during food preparation, toddlers are best off in the safety of a playpen or high chair. Anticipate, too, that when he is learning to walk he will grab anything to steady himself, including hot oven doors and wall heaters. Make sure he cannot reach them. Although he may seem confident in the water, even if he knows how to swim, he still should never be left alone even for a moment. Children have drowned in less than two inches of water, which makes the bathroom a dangerous area.

What makes vigilance so important is that at this age a child is agile enough to get into a lot of trouble. He also is not old enough to remember "no" or to understand the concept of danger when he is exploring.

When it comes to resting from all this activity, by the age of 3 he will usually sleep about 12 hours including one daytime nap. Many toddlers have trouble falling or staying asleep, "fighting" sleep through fear of parental separation or adjustments to toilet training. Here's where a bedtime ritual becomes an effective way of making the transition. Time to wind down from the day, a routine for undressing, washing up, brushing teeth, getting into pajamas and reading bedtime stories all help dissolve the struggle.

Toddlers may find their own ways of comforting themselves into sleep, such as thumb-sucking or cuddling a teddy bear or blanket, banging their heads against the crib or headboard, or rocking their bodies. All are normal within reason. A night-light gives a child assurance and makes checking on him easy for parents.

Preschoolers: Ages 4 to 6.
Lightening fast and increasingly more able, a preschooler can use tools, play games, master tricycles . . . and in the beginning years, fall onto and off of everything! Keep up the vigilance of earlier years, but add new areas to be safety-proofed. She will want to be with you, when you are in other rooms of the house.

Here's where garages should come under scrutiny, kitchens and living rooms should be viewed for potential dangers. Experimenting with matches and imaginative uses for toys all come into play. Establish ground rules for putting away toys, and understanding their use.

A 6-year-old will enjoy taking part in family safety plans so make the child an active participant. Rehearse calling the emergency number and providing the information such as your name and address, in case the child has to take this action. Post the number on the telephones, and make sure your child knows where the number is and which one(s) to use. Engage the child in periodic checks of all fire alarms throughout the house. Go through the actual route of your escape plan (your fire department can help you if you need assistance) from a child's room and other areas and reinforce for your child what to do when the smoke alarm rings. Hold periodic practice drills of what you and she would do in case of a fire. Designate a meeting place where the family will gather after a fire, such as a neighbor's house. All these are good "grown-up" activities that can save lives.

This decorative measuring chart is a fun way to keep track of how much she's grown.

Nursery furniture that is generally lower in height and lighter in scale than other furniture, should comply with safety standards but can have plenty of style nonetheless. The changing table is designed to fit handsomely as a dresser in an older child's room.

While fire can be a real danger, preschoolers often are more concerned with monsters and ghosts, especially at night. Most 4- to 6-year-olds give up daytime naps and sleep 10 1/2 to 11 1/2 hours at night, but experience fear of monsters, anxiety about the dark, waking in the night and reluctance to sleep alone. Disorders of very deep sleep, including bed-wetting, sleepwalking and night terrors, also may develop at this age.

Children experiencing these problems respond well to a low-key approach to night terrors, with assurances and positive support that fears are unfounded. A regular schedule for bedtime and maintaining a night-light will help them through this stage. Guards on the bed can keep sleepwalkers from harming themselves.

Grade-Schoolers: Ages 6 to 12.
Children at this stage form attachments with the outside world. Their focus is on other children. Other adults, such as teachers, become role models in addition to parents. At home, they establish their own worlds, and rooms become their own personal domains, more often than not the activity centers of their increasingly busy social lifes. Frequent socializing with friends, including overnight stays, are handled best by furnishings that can easily accommodate more than one child. While sleeping on a bunk bed is dangerous for a child younger than 6 years old, these arrangements now can help provide stay-over space for kids and friends. Acceptance within the peer group is an important part of the general socializing of a youngster.

Young grade-schoolers sleep solidly for as long as ten hours a night. Any sleep problems seem to be more similar to adult problems for example, insomnia which is often due to of stress and anxiety. The nightmares of earlier years have largely been replaced by peaceful sleep, interrupted only by the occasional bad dream. Children read on their own at this stage, for school and for pleasure. Playing and following sports and other creative activities are extensions of the rapid learning that is going on in school. Many kids develop hobbies and collections of meaningful objects that need to be incorporated into storage and display areas for their living spaces.

Heirloom furniture combines well with modern toys and restrained decorating for a studious child. The wallcovering, an allover abstract pattern, is paired with a plaid fabric on the bed.

Collection Display Case

There are albums for stamps and coins, and shoe boxes for baseball cards, but some things that youngsters collect—like bottle caps or butterflies—are best displayed in a case. This project is easy to make and the dimensions can be varied to fit your child's needs. When finished, the case can be hung or can stand on a table.

1. Cut the Frame Pieces. Cut the pieces for the frame to the size given or to whatever dimensions you like, as long as all measurements are in proportion to the dimensions given. Cut a 1/8" x1/4" dado to the length of each piece, 1/4" in from one edge (see Frame: Edge View). Cut a 1/4" x 1/4" rabbet the length of each piece on the other edge of the same side. Then, miter the corners at a 45-degree angle. Sand the pieces and finish as you wish.

2. Glue the Frame. Run glue along the mitered edge and assemble the frame with the glass in place (for cases with dimensions different from those given, use a piece of glass 1/2" larger in each dimension than the inside dimensions of the frame). Clamp with a picture frame clamp, wipe excess glue with a damp cloth and allow to dry overnight.

3. Mount the Collection. Cut the back to fit the frame you are building. The nature of what you are mounting determines the material used to line the back. If you are mounting butterflies, you will need something such as mat board to push the mounting pins into. If you are mounting bottle caps, which can be glued, you can simply cover the back with a piece of felt. Whatever material you use should be cut to the same size as the back and glued on; then, place a flat weight on it so that it will dry flat. When dry, mount the items to be displayed. When the items are securely attached, secure the back in the rabbet at the back of the frame with 1/2" brass roundhead wood screws. Use the glue sparingly so it won't overflow inside the case—you won't be able to get at it to wipe it away.

4. Hang or Stand the Case. You can hang the display case on the wall with wire and picture hangers. If you want to have the case stand at an angle, attach a back support with a 1/2" butt hinge (see Option A). If you want it to stand up straight, cut the two stand pieces to the proper dimensions (see Option B).

Tools & Materials

- ☐ (2) 3/4" x 2 "x 18" Any Stock (For frame top and bottom)
- ☐ (2) 3/4" x 2" x 18" Any Stock (For frame sides)
- ☐ (1) 1/4" x 17" x 15" Hardboard (For back)
- ☐ Back Lining 15" x 17" (Felt, velvet or mat board)
- ☐ (2) 1/2" x 1½" x 6" Any Stock (For stand pieces)
- ☐ (1) 1/2" x 1" x 6" Scrap (For back support)
- ☐ (1) 17" x 15" Piece of Glass
- ☐ 1/2" Butt Hinge (Optional) ☐ Glue
- ☐ 1/2" Roundhead Wood Screws ☐ Paint or Other Finish
- ☐ Picture Frame Clamps ☐ Wire and Picture Hangers

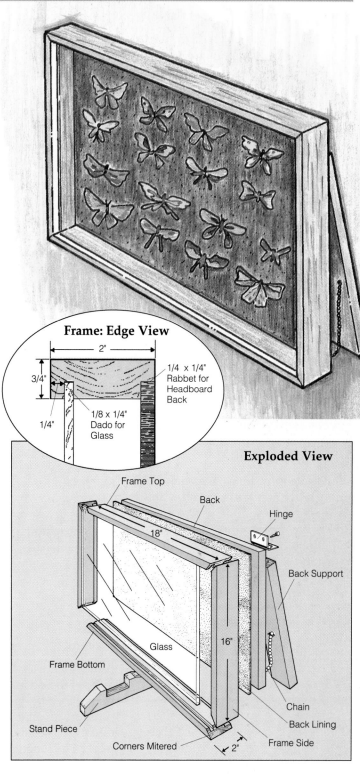

Frame: Edge View

2"

3/4"

1/4"

1/4 x 1/4" Rabbet for Headboard Back

1/8 x 1/4" Dado for Glass

Exploded View

Frame Top

Back

Hinge

18"

Back Support

Frame Bottom

Glass

16"

Chain

Back Lining

Frame Side

Stand Piece

Corners Mitered

2"

Option A: Hinge Stand

1/2" Brass Butt Hinge

1/2 x 2" Wooden Back Support Hinged to Back of Case

Small Chain

Option B: Base

Glue to Stand

Two Required

1½"

6"

1/2"-Thick Material

Ergonomics: Making Furniture Fit

Children are enchanted by scaled furnishings. It makes living within their worlds much less of a Lilliputian mismatch. Children are just as uncomfortable in many adult-sized chairs and tables as adults are in children's furniture. Resolving these differences is a problem, since children outgrow furnishings, do not fit exactly into the same growth patterns as their peers, and can grow sporadically, making it difficult to predict exactly what size they will be at any given age. There is no perfectly proportioned chair, for instance, for a five-year-old. However, within some boundaries, you can estimate the critical dimensions of a child and somewhat predict what size he's likely to become in the next few years and suit your furniture accordingly. Some critical dimensions are total height, level of elbows, distance from back to inside of leg when seated, height from floor to back of knee, etc.

With some furnishings, kids can pretty much adjust to large sizes and then simply grow into them. With others, having furniture that fits is important for learning and health. Work and study areas, electronic centers and furnishings such as desks where a child may use a keyboard and view a screen are particularly important areas to consider scale. Ergonomics, the relationship of a body and its surroundings, offers good guidelines for deciding the best furniture for your child at different stages.

A look at an ergonomic chart shows the wide variety of sizes a child passes through, and how this relates to his work and play surfaces. Here are some suggestions for using the information:

Chairs. Getting a chair a child can grow into is a more practical and comfortable selection than choosing a small chair and continuing to use it after the child has outgrown it. Help adjust the fit early on by adding a back cushion to provide support if the child is too small. Dangling feet are uncomfortable since they cause pinched circulation in the thighs. A step-stool, used as a footrest, under the table can help solve this problem until the child grows. Cushions to raise seat height can extend the useful life of a child's proportioned chair. Attach with Velcro strips to keep them in place.

Tables and Desks. Be sure there is enough clearance underneath the table so that a chair can be pulled up properly. Considerations also include how the work surface relates to the chairs used with it and whether or not the table is convenient as a standing work surface.

Optimum study work surface height is a minimum of 2" to 3" below elbow height. For a craft area where force may be used (like hammering), a lower height is best. You can get a good idea of the best height for your child by measuring her and anticipating her growth (such as seated outer elbow height, seated length from backside to the inside of her knee, etc.).

Although it was difficult to find just a few years ago, adjustable furniture for children recently has come into the market. Included are tables that tilt and change heights as well as chairs modeled after office furniture with adjustable backs and seats.

Other furniture, such as bunk bed and study area combinations, also are adjustable. Some units can be transformed from a crib to a youth bed, and then again to a twin sized bed. Modular units lend themselves to easy reconfiguration that can change dimensions to adapt to a quickly growing child.

In any case, it all starts with an understanding of the ways in which a child will grow. The charts and drawings found on the following page can help determine the most appropriate sizes for new furnishings.

Some furnishings are designed to "grow" with your child. For instance, a crib transforms easily into a youth bed (top), bunk beds are let down for a more mature look (middle), while twin armoires and a twin bed prove to be the perfect size for the young sophisticate (bottom).

Anthropometric Data

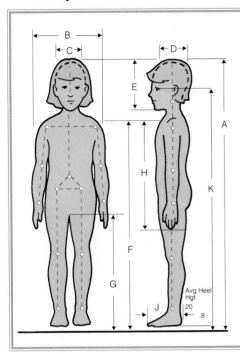

Ages and Sizes. These drawings and the corresponding chart, which shows average dimensions of boys and girls at different ages, are your guides in designing comfortable furniture for children. By studying the chart, you can see how a child's center of gravity becomes lower as the child grows.

Age (years)	Without			With Shoes			
	Birth	**1**	**3**	**5**	**7**	**9**	**12**
Weight (pounds)	7.5	20	29	39	49	59	82
A Standing Height	19.9	28.6	36.7	43.0	48.0	52.0	58.5
B Shoulder Width	6.0	8.0	9.5	10.3	11.3	12.1	13.7
C Head Width	3.8	4.9	5.2	5.4	5.5	5.6	5.7
D Head Length	4.0	6.3	6.9	7.0	7.1	7.3	7.3
E Head Height	5.0	6.9	7.7	7.7	8.0	8.1	8.4
F Shoulder Height	14.9	22.2	28.9	34.1	38.2	42.0	47.5
G Crotch Height	6.6	9.6	14.7	19.3	22.3	24.9	28.7
H Arm Length	7.6	12.0	16.4	18.2	20.7	23.1	25.9
J Foot Length	3.1	4.3	5.6	6.3	7.1	7.8	8.6
K Eye Level	17.4	25.1	32.8	39.1	44.0	48.0	54.5

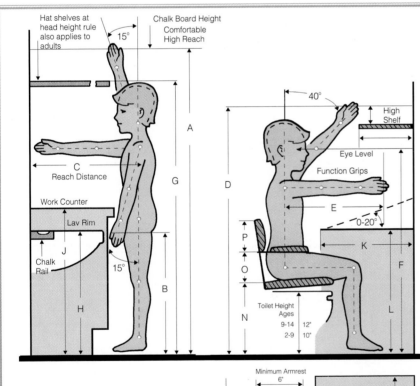

Easy Reaches, Comfy Seating.
Reach varies with age and size. Use this illustration and corresponding chart to guide you in designing storage systems, grooming areas and activity furniture such as easels. School-age seating dimensions are helpful in designing desks and tables. Use the profile and overhead drawings with corresponding charts to design such furniture. Footrests and pillows help smaller bodies fit, allowing for growth with the same furniture pieces.

Up to Age (years)	**5**	**7**	**9**	**12**
A High Reach	47.7	53.9	59.4	67.1
B Low Reach	18.3	20.1	21.8	24.7
C Reach Distance	17.1	19.5	21.7	24.3
D High Reach	36.1	40.0	44.0	49.2
E Reach Radius	15.2	17.5	19.5	21.9
F Eye Level	30.4	33.5	36.5	41.0
G Hat Shelf Height	43.0	48.0	52.0	58.5
H Lavatory Height	19.0	23.0	25.0	27.0
J Work Top	22.5	25.0	27.3	31.3
K Work Depth	13.0	14.0	15.0	16.5
L Table Height	17.5	18.9	20.7	23.3
M Seat Length	9.9	10.8	11.8	13.3
N Seat Height	10.4	11.4	12.8	14.6
O Backrest	4.8	5.1	5.4	5.7
P Backrest Height	5.0	5.1	5.6	6.2
Q Armrest Spacing	12.0	13.0	14.0	16.5
R Seat Width	11.0	12.0	13.0	14.5
S Table Width	21.0	24.0	24.0	28.0

Anthropometric data courtesy of American Institute of Architects

Safety Features for Kids

It's easy to see that different stages create different safety problems in raising children. The sobering facts are that more children are lost to us through accidents than through all illnesses combined! The National Safety Council as well as a number of industry groups have brought a strong focus to this problem; but it can't be emphasized enough.

Fires and Burns. Next to automobiles, these are the second most common causes of childhood deaths. Never leave young children alone. Practice fire prevention. Check cords, install and maintain smoke detectors, turn pot handles so that they don't protrude from ranges, have dry fire extinguishers in the kitchen, and religiously lock up flammable materials that might tempt a child (such as paint solvents in a garage home workshop). Keep cups away from edges; don't place them on mats or tablecloths that a toddler can grab, overturning hot liquid on himself. Renew extension cords and cover outlet covers. Never have an open socket without a bulb, even a dead one. Check that curtains and other materials will not blow against heat-producing sources such as fireplaces or heaters. Turn your water heater thermostat down to 120-125°F to avoid any chance of scalding a child. Unplug small appliances such as blowdryers when not in use and keep out of a child's reach.

Drowning. A child can drown in just 2" of water or less. Children should never be left alone in tubs. Do not leave youngsters unattended near swimming pools, ponds, hot tubs, and when young, toilets, diaper pails and showers. Most kids adore water from an early age and have no idea of its danger.

It's always important to be prepared. A standaway portable escape ladder goes rigid when you step on it and won't buckle or sway. It comes in two-story and three-story lengths.

Attractive smoke detectors in designs kids love are part of the goal to make sure that all nurseries are equipped with alarms.

Safety gates keep toddlers away from dangerous areas and are installed and removed with ease. Consider using them at kitchen and bath doorways to keep children away from water as well as at the top and bottom of stairways.

Contemporary balconies and lofts with screening are safe for kids. It's important that openings between banisters are no wider than crib standards, or no more than 2 ³/₈" apart. Screening will fill the gap if the railing doesn't.

Home Furnishing Safety Standards

Government agencies and industry regulatory groups have combined to establish a number of standards for children's furnishings. As you may have noticed, new standards constant-ly are being introduced as new products and their potential problems become known. Included here are some established areas of concern.

Do-it-yourselfers should pay particular attention to the safety standards that apply to modern furnishings and make sure that any projects they make for their offspring are at least as safe. Use the industry awareness to set your do-it-yourself standards. For instance, current regulations in crib safety make it mandatory that corner posts be no higher than 1/16" above the end of the panel. No custom design should ignore such sound advice. Also use current standards in deciding whether a secondhand or even hand-me-down antique furnishing is safe.

While the standards are not always definitive because variations in materials, construction and design cannot be standardized, industry and government groups do specify the areas of concern.

The Juvenile Products Manufacturers Association (JPMA), is a group of concerned manufacturers of nursery and other baby products. It has put into place a Product Safety Certification Program based on testing standards that have been published for each product category by an independent group, the American Society for Testing and Materials (ASTM). This highly-respected, nonprofit organization develops standards through committees that have a balance of industry and consumer repre-sentatives. The JPMA Safety Certification testing ensures that the products you have selected with the approval were built and designed with safety in mind. To qualify, manufacturers have initial tests conducted by the Detroit Testing Laboratory according to the ASTM standards. Once certified, manu-facturers continue with quarterly product testing. The testing lab meets annually with each manufacturer to monitor testing procedures.

Evaluation is based on general structure, performance, labeling and warning statements. During the tests, products and all their parts are pushed and pulled, horizontally and vertically, with a great deal more stress than they would undergo in normal use. You can ask retailers if the product you are considering is certified, or look for the certification mark on the product. The Juvenile Products Manufacturers Association Certification seal assures that the product has met the association's standards.

JUVENILE PRODUCTS MANUFACTURERS ASSOCIATION

CERTIFIED

AN INDEPENDENT TESTING LABORATORY VALIDATES THE MANUFACTURER'S CERTIFICATION OF THIS CRIB TO ASTM F-1169 AND F-966

What follows are qualities reviewed in the testing standards for various juvenile products from JPMA:

High Chairs. Strength, stability and security of occupant, through broad base, waist and crotch straps that are independent of the tray. Tray that locks securely. If folding, chair has a locking device to keep chair from collapsing.

Portable Hook-on Chairs. Secure means to attach to the table and lock it on, restraint system to secure the child, no caps or plugs which can be pulled off. Never secure this chair in a place where a child can push off with his feet.

Play Pens. Holes and mesh openings designed not to catch fingers, toes or buttons (less than 1/4" openings), securely fastened to strong rails and floor.

Carriages and Strollers. Stability, strength and effective brakes; a latching device that prevents accidental folding; seat belt and crotch strap secured to frame; brakes that securely lock wheels; shopping basket low and located directly over or in front of real wheels.

Infant Walkers. Stability against tipping and construction that does not entrap feet or hands.

Gates and Expandable Enclosures. Strong top rails and framing components and openings too small to trap a child's head (if V or diamond shapes, these should be no more than $1\frac{1}{2}$" across).

Full-Size Cribs. No corner posts (less that 1/16" above the end panel); crib slats spaced no more than $2\frac{3}{8}$" apart; strong components that will not loosen (including the slats).

While it is not possible to totally predict a child's moves into and out of safety during the growing years, by using these guidelines, the most common dangers can be eliminated. For further information, check the references found at the end of this book. These organizations are up to date on the most recent safety programs and facts.

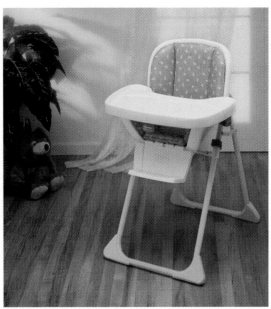

Rounded corners are incorporated into the design of this contemporary child's youth-tester bed and coordinated night table and desk unit. Note the mirror behind the headrest of the bed, adding to the open look of the room.

Latchkey children or any kids who might be at home alone will feel and be safer with a video to let them know who is outside.

Additional Safety Recommendations

■ Never compromise on crib safety features. According to the Consumer Product Safety Commission, more infants die in accidents involving cribs than any other nursery product.

■ A crib mattress should fit snugly with no more than two fingers width between the edge of the mattress and the crib side.

■ Check cribs for sturdy construction and stability. Avoid exposed screws, bolts or fasteners with sharp edges or points; avoid scissor-like mechanisms or exposed springs that could crush fingers and avoid openings that could entrap a baby's head.

■ Toys strung across a crib should be removed when an infant can push up on hands and knees (about 5 months of age).

■ Never place cribs near drapery or blind cords where a child could become entangled and strangle on them. Be concerned with these dangers once toddlers begin crawling.

■ Use infant walkers only under supervision and block stairways. Throw rugs, raised thresholds and carpet edges can cause walkers to tip over. Add bumpers to keep walkers from going through doorways.

■ Safety straps for high chairs, strollers and changing tables that are easy to fasten and unfasten help assure they will be used.

■ Infant bedding, stuffed toys and other soft furnishings should be used with care due to the risk of suffocation.

■ Pillows are decor items only and are not intended for infant's use since they can cause suffocation. Keep them out of cribs, play yards, bassinets and carriages.

■ Crib bumper pads protect a baby's head, and should fit around the entire crib. Tie or snap securely into place and have straps on both the upper and lower edges.

■ Bumper straps should be trimmed of any excess length after secured, to prevent the baby from chewing on the straps or becoming entangled and strangling.

■ Remove and do not use bumper pads once the baby can pull up to a standing position so the baby cannot use the pads to try to climb out of the crib. The same applies to stuffed toys.

■ New and used cribs should be checked to assure that drop side latches cannot be easily released by an infant and that the mattress is securely attached to the head and footboard.

■ The mattress should be the same size as the crib so there are no gaps to catch arms or legs. The minimum rail height should be 22" from top of railing to mattress set at the lowest level. The sides, when lowered, should be 4" above the mattress. Never leave the rails down when a baby is in the crib.

■ Common danger areas of older cribs include corner posts that are greater than 1/16" above the end panel and may cause entanglement with clothing; decorative cutouts between corner posts and rail that may entrap a child's head; missing slats or slats spaced wider than 2⅜"; painted or finished parts that may contain lead; decals or other decorations on the interior that could cause choking.

■ Lower the crib mattress before the baby can sit unassisted. Have it at its lowest level before the baby can stand.

■ Use netting or safe extenders on top of cribs for babies who try to climb out.

■ Switch to a bed as soon as a child reaches 35" in height, or as soon as he has learned how to climb out of the crib (usually at 2 or 3 years of age).

■ After switching to a bed, use detachable safety rails to discourage climbing, to prevent falls and to make your child feel more secure.

■ Do not allow children under 6 to climb into upper bunk beds. Make sure that the upper bunk guard rail is truly adequate; it must be at least 5" above the mattress to act as an effective barrier.

■ In the house at large, keep plastic wrap and plastic dry cleaning bags away from children since they can cling to a baby's face and cause suffocation. Babies should never be allowed to lie face down or sleep on cushions, soft adult comforters or blankets, pillows, plush rugs or other soft areas that might interfere with breathing. Unattended, a child can quickly roll off an adult bed.

■ Do not tie pacifiers or other items around a baby's neck, since cords and ribbons can catch on things or become twisted and cause strangling.

■ Ban poisonous plants and flowers from your home (some examples; caladium, diefenbachia, philodendron, English ivy, mistletoe, poinsettia and rhododendron).

■ Consider a child's low chair and table instead of a high chair as soon as possible. Increase high chair safety by being sure the base is broad and weighted so it won't tip, that it has a harness that will hold a climbing baby, and that a latch keeps the baby from moving the tray.

■ Make sure that all paint your child encounters is lead free. Be especially suspect of older furniture and even moldings on older homes. Keep abreast of current government safety levels and standards and recommendations for both testing and safe removal. You can contact the National Safety Council for updated information at (312) 527-4800.

Shaker Stool Project

This classic pine stool will remain a cherished heirloom long after your child is grown. Providing such a stool empowers a child to act on her own. Paint it or stain it, and add self-adhesive strips to the treads (available at home centers) to prevent slippage.

Tools & Materials

- A (2) 3/4" x 14 1/2" x 19 1/4" (For sides)
- B (1) 3/4" x 7 1/4" x 21" (For top step)
- C (1) 3/4" x 6 3/4" x 21" (For bottom step)
- D (4) 7/8" x 2" x 20" (For stretchers)
- Router and 1/4" Radius Bit (Optional)
- No. 10 Roundhead Brass Wood Screws

- Carpenter's Glue
- Sandpaper
- Screwdriver

Exploded View

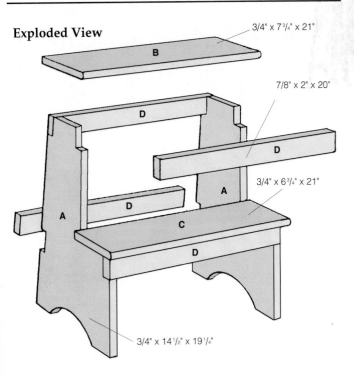

3/4" x 7 3/4" x 21"

7/8" x 2" x 20"

3/4" x 6 3/4" x 21"

3/4" x 14 1/2" x 19 1/4"

Side View

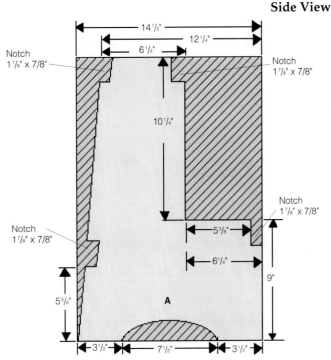

1. Cut the Sides. Measure 12 1/2" from the front edge of the top, mark and cut a taper along the back edge. Next cut a 7 1/2" scallop along the bottom edge, leaving two 3 1/2" feet for the stool to stand upon.

2. Cut Out the Step. Measure 6 1/4" from the back of the top edge (see Side View). Then measure straight down the board 10 1/4". On the front edge, measure up from the bottom 9" and mark. Next measure across 6 1/4" where the line should intersect at a right angle with the line drawn from the top. Cut along the lines and sand the edges.

3. Notch for the Stretchers. Cut four notches to hold the stretchers. On either side of the top, cut notches 1 7/8" deep x 7/8" wide. Cut the same size notch on the front edge of the bottom step. Finally, cut the same size notch 5 5/8" from the bottom of the back edge.

4. Sand All Parts. All of the parts must be thoroughly sanded.

5. Attach the Stretchers. Use glue and two brass screws for each joint and attach.

6. Fit the Steps. Round the edges of the steps with a 1/4" radius bit or by sanding. Fit the steps so that they overhang the edges, front and sides, by 1/2". Attach the steps using glue and four brass screws.

7. Finish the Stool. This piece may be finished in many ways. Use your imagination.

Project Courtesy of Georgia-Pacific Corp.

Basic Furnishings

There's something very appealing about most children's furniture, especially the sweet furnishings for a nursery. From baby quilts to bassinets, each new acquisition brings with it all the excitement of new parenthood. With practical and safety considerations addressed, what's left is the sheer joy of selecting the furniture that will become part of your family's treasures. Here's your chance to be as fanciful or practical as you wish.

One enormous advantage you have today is that there are a number of stores and kid's furnishing manufacturers vying for your dollar. This translates into a greater selection of both styles and prices. Included in this section are a number of do-it-yourself kid's furniture projects suitable for newborns and older. Read the savvy pointers found here before you head out to the shopping malls or to pick up the necessary tools.

Furniture necessities will change depending upon the age and stage of your child. With the great diversity of scaled furnishings on the market these days you will not have any trouble matching the decor with that of the rest of your home (if that is what you are after) or creating a brand new look and feel tailored to the young resident.

Defining Your Needs

Think through your furnishing needs from the very beginning. Furniture used for a baby, if wisely selected, will be suitable for the same child's room as he grows.

Nursery Necessities

Initially, babies need very little furniture. A crib, some kind of changing and dressing center, storage units for toiletries and clothes, a place for a parent to comfortably sit to cuddle and feed the infant, a bathing center (often in the bathroom), lights, a baby sound monitor, and baby carriers cover the basics.

You may need to store strollers, walkers and carriers in this room if you don't have additional space elsewhere in your home. If you give over the closet to bulky storage of items such as these, you may find that freestanding storage units are even more convenient for baby clothes, towels, blankets and the like.

What's the best place for your baby's room? Answers may surprise you. One family, living in an apartment without a separate room to convert,

transformed the master suite's dressing room into a nursery. This provided a separate space for the baby, which proved far more convenient than blocking off a corner of the bedroom with a screen or temporary partition. The baby's belongings were kept centralized, while parents did not have to worry about noises keeping the baby awake, since she was in her own room. Armoires in the master bedroom took over the storage load for the grown-ups, since they had lost the closet. By the time the baby had outgrown the nursery, the parents were ready to move to larger quarters.

Be as creative in your own planning, and you may find exciting new solutions. In addition, consider these factors in defining your needs.

Redefining Rooms. Which area should be the nursery? Do you have a specific room earmarked, or do you need to rethink your home's layout?

Length of Stay. Do you plan to stay in this house for many years? Conversely, is it more likely you will move within five years? Developing a furniture-to-fit scheme or using built-ins makes good sense if you

have long-term plans to stay in your current home. If the room will belong to the child for most of his childhood, plan progressive purchases at the beginning. Select multipurpose furniture that merely needs to be added to as the child grows. The finished floor plan should include future furniture needs to make sure everything will fit, then you can scale it back to current needs. For instance, if you eventually will have bunk beds in the room, you may need to limit the size of the dressers you purchase now so they will fit later.

Style. Do you have strong design tastes? Follow them for your children's room furnishings. The room's decor shouldn't be a total departure from the rest of the house. You'll be spending considerable time in this room, at least in the beginning. There's almost as much variety in styles for children's furniture as for adult counterparts. White and colored modern pieces, traditional country styles, Early American inspired designs, Shaker simplicity and mellow oak wood-grain styles are just some of the selections available.

Furniture Colors. Wood furniture tones go with almost any other colors you might select. However, some furniture, especially the tubular steel or some of the basic white easy-care pieces, come with colored drawer fronts or accent parts. In selecting this furniture, ask yourself if the accent hue can be changed without totally replacing

School-age children are old enough to have collected a number of toys and to have interests that require storage and workspace. Here, custom cabinetry with laminate covering outfit this pretty girl's room.

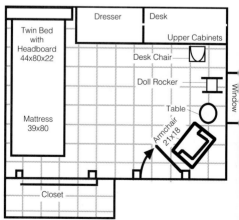

A novelty youth bed is just right for a preschooler, sure to make her feel special. This room has been designed in such a way that it will easily adapt to school-age furniture additions when the time comes.

Brilliant bedcoverings are a natural choice for a bright and active child, once she starts expressing preferences of her own. Note the circus-theme headboard and window treatment.

the furniture, and if you and the child will enjoy the look you have selected. Will this room seem jarring and out of place compared to the rest of your furnishings? If you answered yes to the last question, you probably don't really like the furniture deep down. You deserve to like the furniture as much as your kids do.

Mix and Match. You do not have to keep to one style in any room. Eclectic mixing of furniture allows you to incorporate the best of the practical with stylish furnishings as well. This opens the door for secondhand furnishings, garage sale finds and antique store gems. Just be sure older furnishings conform to the safety standards established for today. Do not paint over old paint unless you are sure that the old is lead-free; strip the furniture and start over from scratch instead.

Preschool Needs

There comes a time when a baby moves out of the crib into a bed and the room becomes a playroom. Convertible cribs that become small beds are available and you may opt to purchase one of these. Otherwise, purchase a twin bed with a guard rail on one or both sides. This type of bed is safe for the child and provides a comfortable spot for adults to read to him.

A child-size table and chairs are useful additions for the more active child. Adjustable tables and chairs will span the growth period for 3- to 6-year-olds. A miniature rocker or hobby horse can provide an outlet for a bundle of energy, as can a range of action toys. Playhouses or other make-believe implements need to be included, along with storage for increased toys that come with this age.

Toddlers will climb on virtually anything. Check that furniture will not topple over from a young explorer's weight, and consider bolting bookcases and such to walls as a precaution. An adult chair, especially a rocker, remains a useful adjunct for providing a place to cuddle, read to a child or just to relax while you share time. Check adult-size chairs as well as children's size furniture to make sure that the base is wide enough to inhibit tipping.

Redecorating. When you redecorate a child's room (adding furnishings for a preschooler, rearranging for a young student,

revamping for a preteen, etc.), include the child in the decisions. From the start, lay out the parameters as to how much change you (and the budget) will allow. By establishing the extent of the redecorating from the beginning expectations are kept in line with reality.

Personalizing a secondhand furniture piece with vim and vigor enables it to fit in almost anywhere, as this comic-page decoupaged chest demonstrates.

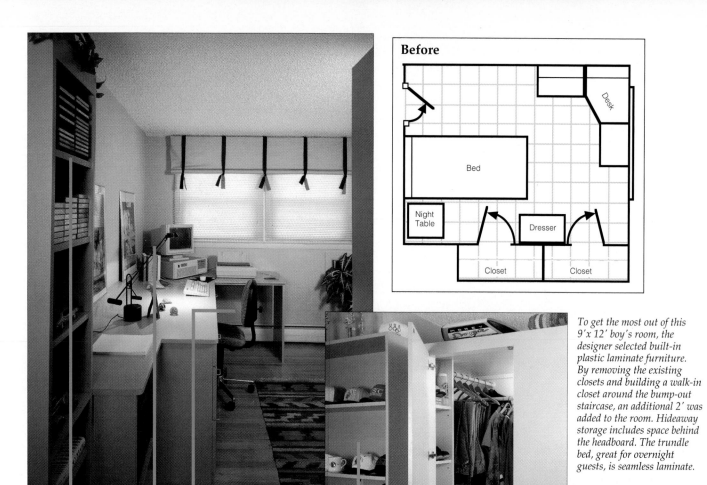

Desk

Bed

Night Table

Dresser

Closet

Closet

To get the most out of this 9' x 12' boy's room, the designer selected built-in plastic laminate furniture. By removing the existing closets and building a walk-in closet around the bump-out staircase, an additional 2' was added to the room. Hideaway storage includes space behind the headboard. The trundle bed, great for overnight guests, is seamless laminate.

Ergonomic Desk Chair

Bookshelf Headboard

Work Desk with Computer Equipment

Clothes Closet with Organizer Shelving

Shelf Storage for CD's and Cassettes

Trundle Bed

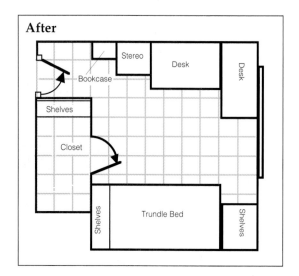

After

Stereo

Desk

Desk

Bookcase

Shelves

Closet

Shelves

Trundle Bed

Shelves

By the time your child reaches preschool, he will have developed some strong personality traits that should be considered when decorating. Is your child a neatness fanatic who likes a specific place for everything? Would open shelving with everything in view suit your child's freewheeling spirit better? Are lengthy projects your child's delight, making undisturbed table space a special need?

The floor itself becomes a major play space for a preschooler. Consider devoting part of the budget to comfortable and easily cleaned wood or resilient flooring. While the floor will continue to be a major play space for a child from this age forward, the child will need his own specific furniture to accommodate school-age work and play.

Grade-School Essentials

A school-age child's room must fulfill many needs; specifically study, sociability, solitude and sports.

Study. At the top of the furniture list is a good study-desk that is properly lighted. Be prepared to have this desk transformed into a media center, where electronic games as well as keyboard-accessed computer units may become a needed part of the learning environment. For any electric keyboard unit, lighting and proper desk and chair related height are important. Growing backs need support as do young wrists. Consider, too, locating a desk where a computer screen will not pick up glare from windows or other light sources (see the lighting section for further information).

Sociability. Overnight guests can be accommodated in a variety of ways, from fold-out bed and chairs to inflatable mattresses to trundle beds or an extra bunk. Since school-age is the beginning of sociability, prepare for it by providing the necessary means for your child to have friends over. Is your child the kind who has many projects and likes to share them? A good choice for him might be a large-size table with comfortable stools or chairs for sharing projects. You may want to consider bookshelf space for reference materials and your child's own book collections.

Sports. In addition to equipments, memorabilia need to be stored or displayed by a youthful sports enthusiast. Shelves for trophies and storage units for equipment will fill the bill. Exercise equipment and an ample space to use it in are becoming increasingly important for children who may not fill their needs for activity within the school system.

Solitude. A comfortable chair is conducive to dreaming and planning, both major activities for schoolchildren. Provide the chair with a good reading light, and you can create a corner that is perfect for young readers. Letting a child of school-age actively take part in the design of her room helps ensure that the room is a haven for her growing years. It also shows your respect for her taste and wishes. After all, it's the one place where she can retreat and be completely in control of her space. In her room, she is her own master, free to be whatever and whomever she pleases. Such solitude is necessary for healthy growth.

Here's a place to daydream about all the adventures of being a modern environmentalist or jungle child.

Smart Furniture Buying

Kid's room furniture can be found in a number of stores, each with its special appeal. Juvenile stores generally have products for the child from newborn through crib-age, and may or may not handle furnishings beyond that stage. Often, these specialty stores carry everything from soft goods, such as sheets and bedding, to furniture.

Furniture that's made for children, crib-age on up (as well as some juvenile furnishings), can be found in specialty stores, department stores, general furniture stores, furniture galleries, and mail-order catalogues. A number of interior designers create built-in designs for children, and do-it-yourselfers make their own children's furniture as well.

If you have a favorite adult furniture manufacturer or gallery, start your shopping there. Many companies are adding children's lines that will be entirely compatible with your other furnishings. If you are making a major investment, check out an

A crib and changing table plus space to store clothing changes are basically all you need for a newborn.

unknown retailer with the Better Business Bureau in your area or other local consumer protection agencies in your area. And don't overlook the "parents" network, invaluable, for finding great sources for all kids' needs.

Perfect Fit. "Youth" furniture sounds as though it is a distinct category, but it is not. Generally, youth furniture is also merchandised as correlate groups which are smaller in scale than average furniture. As such, the furniture may be sold with twin or bunk beds for use by children and also have double- and queen-size beds to match. In some smaller spaces for adults these days, (and for guest rooms and the like) the same furniture is ideal. Another space-saving feature of youth groups is that often suites of furniture are designed to work in a "wrap" design, around a corner to make the most of available wall space. Various components, including dressers, open shelving, bookcases, hutches, desks, corner desks, all can be lined up in a space-saving way. The advantage of this furniture over built-ins is that it can be disassembled and reconfigured within the same room or moved with the family and set up in a new space.

Another type of furniture grouping includes units that build upwards, incorporating study lofts and sleeping areas within architectural-looking structures. Many of these also can be redesigned to meet a growing child's needs.

Streamlined white furnishings have all the elements you need, and work well together in any configuration. The ready-to-assemble ensemble has many well-thoughtout pieces, including this child's armoire.

Furniture Qualities

Wood furniture can be as confusing as the forest and the trees. It can be judged by the finish and detailing of its construction, with the same quality pointers as adult furniture. Look for dust panels between drawers, dovetailing, reinforcement of corners, overall smoothness with no rough sanding, professional finishing, reinforcement with screws and nails instead of staples.

Laminated finishes may masquerade as wood and be combined with solid wood as well. For instance, dresser surfaces and desk tops may be laminated to provide a rough and tough easy-care surface while sides may be solid wood; shelves may be laminated or veneered particleboard or plywood to provide dimensional stability and no warping, and backboards may be of a particle-board with a laminate or veneer. Ask salesmen what advantages there are for these materials in a specific application in construction; often they are practical in use as well as easy on the purse. For instance, a desktop may warp and rock less when made of composite materials than when made of solid wood. Solid woods may be used for edges and aprons to give a "natural" look.

Metal furniture, particularly for all-in-one bunk and desk units, often is specifically designed to accommodate the special needs of children. Quality pointers to look for include sturdiness of the materials, substantial quality of all parts, ability to withstand roughhousing without loosening any fastening devices and easy upkeep.

With all furniture that is designed to be used in component parts, make sure that there's an easy-to-use system to level the units and attach them together. Invite your child to test out the store units, and do the same yourself. Be sure that drawers have stops that keep them from pulling out. Bang and pull drawers and check that they work solidly, snugly in their frames and smoothly. Shelves should fit snugly as well, and if adjustable, should stay in place once positioned but be easy to relocate. See how easy it is to get into an upper bunk, and be sure that the unit provides enough space both top and bottom. Check desk units for compatibility with modern electronics, which means some easy way of hooking up electronic equipment with accommodations for electrical cords.

Inspect the areas that are not exposed to get a good idea of the workmanship employed. Messy and unfinished staining and sloppy gluing are both signs of shoddy workmanship.

Don't be a soft touch when it comes to bedding and upholstery, either. Look for easy-care finishes in both, such as Scotchgard, Teflon or Wear-Dated labels, buy quality and demand comfort. A chair that you use with a newborn, if well constructed, will last through an entire childhood. With protective finishes, you can wipe up those unavoidable spills and the upholstery often will remain spotless.

There are novelty furniture pieces that you can buy for a lark, if that suits your style. Beds designed as old shoes, simulating racing cars and even aerie bowers with intertwined twig framing and flowers are treasures to cherish. So are storage units decorated to look like castles, Victorian mansions or farm animals. Furniture pieces as well as other areas of a child's room lend themselves to individuality and spirit.

Before you embark on a furniture buying sortie, know both your budget requirements and your needs. We've included a worksheet and design template (Appendixes A and B). The Budget and Plan Worksheet is set up so you can prioritize furnishings from immediate to future needs. And be sure that you know all the dimensions of the room, your tentative floor plan, and allowances for such clearances as bed making, opening drawers, pulling out chairs and the like.

Whatever your choice, know that the furniture will be long remembered as a scene from childhood.

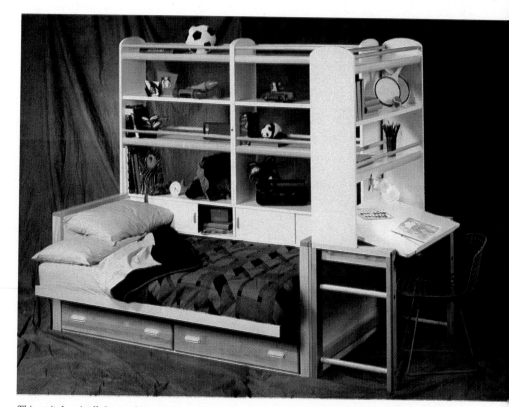

This unit does it all. It even has a bed that pulls out at night and then recedes to become a sofa during the day.

Early American Baby-Changing Cabinet and Tray

This handsome unit has a historical look and can be made from a number of types of wood, including plywood, clear pine, cherry and oak. Finished with a traditional stain such as cherry or oak, this piece will delight anyone. You can give it a decidedly country look by selecting either a milk-paint stain (such as a Shaker blue or barn red), or using a clear stain and polyurethane to finish it. A pickled finish creates a light look or use a sunset color to give it Southwestern flair.

Those who prefer a casual look can use stencils, decals or painted motifs. If you use decals, place them on the exterior only so the baby can't possibly pull them off. It goes without saying that the stains and paints used must be lead-free and non-toxic.

While changing table mattresses and straps are pretty standard, it's a good idea to purchase these items before you start the project to make sure you can have a proper fit. You may want to alter the tray dimensions within 2" or 3" limits in each direction.

Tools & Materials

Cabinet Base

- [ ] A (1) 3/4" x 17 3/4" x 33 1/2" (For top)
- [ ] B (2) 3/4" x 17" x 33 1/2" (For sides)
- [ ] C (1) 3/4" x 13 1/2" x 31 1/4" (For half shelf)
- [ ] D (1) 3/4" x 16 3/4" x 31 1/4" (For full shelf)
- [ ] E (1) 3/4" x 16" x 31 1/4" (For bottom)
- [ ] F (1) 3/4" x 3 1/2" x 32" (For front foot)
- [ ] G (1) 3/4" x 1 3/4" x 31 1/4" (For bottom cross member)
- [ ] H (1) 3/4" x 1 1/4" x 31 1/4" (For top cross member)
- [ ] J (2) 3/4" x 3/4" x 14 1/2" (For top braces)
- [ ] K (1) 3/4" x 3/4" x 30 1/2" (For top back cross member)
- [ ] L (1) 1/4" x 30 3/4" x 31 1/4" Plywood (For back)
      (Faced both sides to match remaining wood)

Cabinet Doors

- [ ] M (4) 3/4" x 2" x 17 3/8" (For stiles)
- [ ] N (4) 3/4" x 2" x 11 5/8" (For rails)
- [ ] P (2) 1/4" x 11 11/16" x 14 7/8" (For panels)

Cabinet Hardware

- [ ] (2) Brass Knobs
- [ ] (2) Magnetic Catches
- [ ] 4d Finishing Nails
- [ ] 1" Brads
- [ ] Felt Strips
- [ ] (2 Pair) Decorating Hinges
- [ ] No.8 x 1 1/4" Flathead Wood Screws

Tray

- [ ] Q (1) 3/4" x 5 11/16" x 34 3/4" (For back)
- [ ] R (2) 3/4" x 5 11/16" x 20 3/8" (For sides)
- [ ] S (1) 3/4" x 6 5/8" x 35 1/2" (For front)
- [ ] T (1) 3/8" x 19 7/8" x 34 5/8" (For bottom)

Tray Hardware

- [ ] 4d Finishing Nails
- [ ] Felt Strips
- [ ] Metal Mending Strips (Optional)

Changing Cabinet

This cabinet keeps baby's needs right at hand. The angled tray provides plenty of room for the baby. The cabinet project takes medium skills in woodworking and requires no subassemblies beyond constructing the doors. The tray is somewhat more difficult; the angle cuts required must be made with precision.

Exploded View

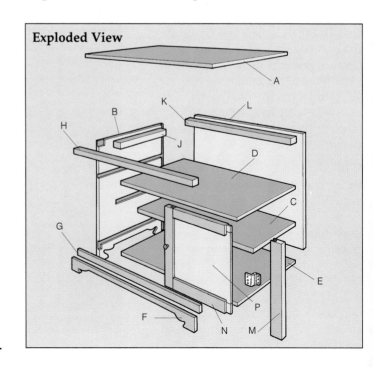

Front View

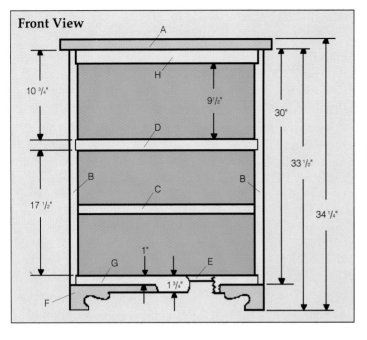

Top View

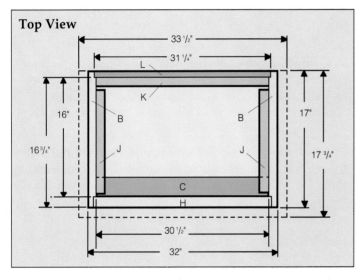

Side Layout

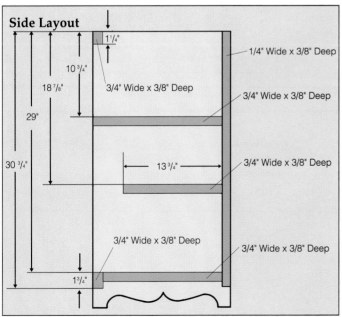

1/4" Wide x 3/8" Deep

3/4" Wide x 3/8" Deep

3/4" Wide x 3/8" Deep

3/4" Wide x 3/8" Deep

3/4" Wide x 3/8" Deep

3/4" Wide x 3/8" Deep

1. Machine the Top. Cut the top (A) to size and round the upper edge on all four sides with a 3/8" quarter-round router bit.

2. Machine the Shelves. Cut both full and half shelves (D & C) to size. Machine half shelf with a standard flush cut 3/8" wide and 3/4" deep (see Standard Flush Cut).

Standard Flush Cut

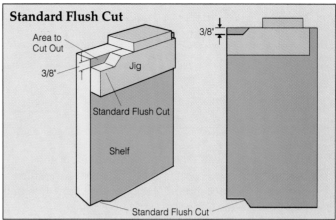

Area to Cut Out

Jig

3/8"

Standard Flush Cut

Shelf

3/8"

Standard Flush Cut

3. Machine the Sides. The two sides (B) are machined with dadoes and flush back rabbets (see Dadoes and Flush-Back Rabbet) on inside faces to produce a mirror-image pair. Cut a pattern to create feet.

Dadoes

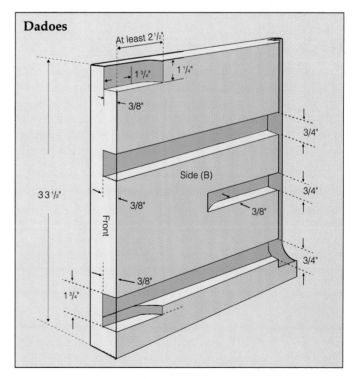

At least 2½"

1 ¾"

1 ¼"

3/8"

3/4"

Side (B)

3/4"

3/8"

3/8"

33½"

Front

3/8"

3/4"

1 ¾"

Flush-Back Rabbet

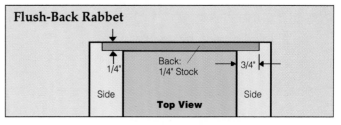

1/4"

Back: 1/4" Stock

3/4"

Side

Side

Top View

4. Machine the Front Foot. Cut the front foot to size. Either cut out a traditional foot pattern (see Scalloped Foot) or leave it solid. Round the top leading edge of the front foot with a 3/8" radius quarter-round router bit.

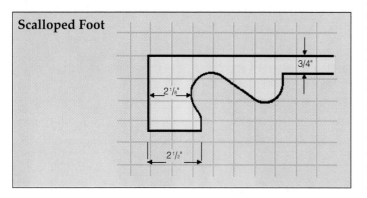

Scalloped Foot

5. Cut the Door Parts. The cabinet's two doors are constructed with a 1/2" center pane (P). Groove the stiles (F) and rails (G) (see Standard Door Construction). Cut both the back panel of the cabinet and the door panels. Use plywood faced on both sides with the same wood used for the rest of the cabinet since it will show when the cabinet doors are open.

6. Sand the Pieces. Rough- and finish-sand the upper surface of the top and both surfaces of the sides. The half shelf, shelf and bottom need only be rough-sanded. Rough- and finish-sand the routed edge of the front foot; the face need only be rough-sanded. Plywood pieces will not need sanding.

7. Assemble the Cabinet. Apply wood glue to the ends of the half shelf, shelf, cross members and bottom, and spread it into the grooves for the pieces that fit into the sides. Fit the parts into the sides and then from underneath the shelves and bottom nail into the sides with 4d finishing nails. Clamp the assembly and check for square, adjusting if necessary. When square, allow the glue to dry.

8. Assemble the Doors. Rough-sand the front, back, inside and outside edges of the stiles and rails (don't sand the grooves). To assemble a door, you will need a very flat piece of 3/4" plywood slightly wider than the door, newspaper to cover the plywood, two pipe clamps, a

straight piece of scrap wood to serve as a spacer, and four C-clamps with pads to protect the wood.

Start the assembly by spreading glue on the tongues of the rails with a brush (wipe away any excess before continuing). Also squeeze a little glue into the groove in the stiles, where the tongues of the rails will sit.

Place two stiles on the ends of a rail. Slip the panel into place and fit the remaining rail in place. Set this assembly onto the piece of plywood covered with newspapers. The assembly sits on top of the plywood, which is on top of the two pipe clamps. The spacer sits on the panel between one edge of the door and the clamps so that the clamps can tighten against the door while the door remains entirely on the plywood. Fingertip tighten the pipe clamps and check for square. If the door is not square, loosen the clamps and make the necessary adjustments.

When the door is square, place a C-clamp with protective pads on each of the four joints at the corners so that the door is clamped to the plywood panel beneath it. This flattens the door against the panel and forces it to be flat, square and perfect. When the doors are set up, remove and finish-sand.

9. Complete the Cabinet. Attach the front foot to the cabinet with glue and No. 8 x 1¼" flathead wood screws. Countersink the screws and cover with screw plugs. Attach the top braces with No. 8 x 1¼" wood screws driven through the braces into the sides.

Place the top upside down on a padded surface and invert the cabinet assembly onto it, back edge flush with back of the sides and centered side to side. Attach the cabinet to the top with countersunk No. 8 x 1¼" flathead wood screws driven through the braces.

Install the doors with hardware lining up so that the tops of hinge pins line up with the inner edge of the rail.

Install the knob halfway down the rail. Place the magnetic-catch close to the doorknob or at top of the drawer.

Check for smooth operation and fit. Mark hardware so you know which part goes where when you remove them.

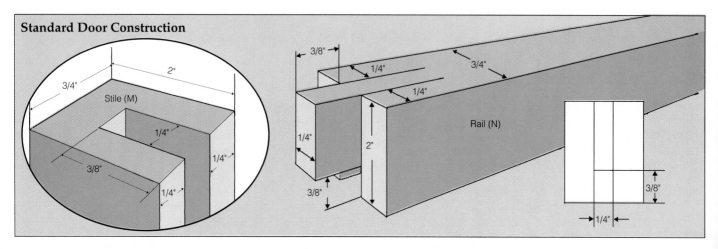

Standard Door Construction

Stile (M)

Rail (N)

Changing Tray

1. Machine the Back. Cut the back (Q) to size. Then, cut a groove 3/8" wide by 3/8" deep 3/4" from bottom edge (see Back Layout).

2. Machine the Sides. Cut the two sides (R) to size, then cut a 3/4" rabbet along the back end of each side (see Side Layout). Cut a 1/4" wide by 3/8" deep groove 3/4" from the bottom of each side on the same face. Finally, cut the front end of each side at a 70-degree angle.

3. Machine the Front. Cut the front to size. Cut a rabbet 3/4" wide and 3/8" deep in both ends (see Front Layout). Next, make 20-degree cuts in the top and bottom edges of the front (see Side View of Front Layout). Finally, cut a groove (at 70-degrees) 1/4" wide and 3/8" deep across the inside face of the front.

4. Sand the Parts. Rough and finish-sand the flat sides.

5. Assemble the Tray. Place the back on a flat work surface, inside face up (see Exploded View). Put glue in the end rabbets and fit the sides to the back. Secure with 4d finishing nails. Set nails and fill holes with wood putty.

Slip the bottom into the grooves along the sides and slide it into the groove in the back (see Top View). Do not glue the bottom in the grooves. Put glue in the rabbets on the ends of the front and set it into position on the ends of the sides. Secure the front with 4d finishing nails, set the nails and fill the holes with wood putty. Then, square up the tray and clamp with padded clamps. Let tray dry.

6. Sand the Joints. Smooth all glue joints and top surfaces of the tray with a sander, then fine finish-sand the interior. Glue strips of felt to the bottom edges to protect the cabinet top from scratches. You may want to use mending plates to secure the tray to the cabinet.

7. Finish Bottom Cabinet and Tray. Remove cabinet doors and finish all parts. Attach cabinet back panel with 1" brads, and attach cabinet doors and hardware.

Exploded View

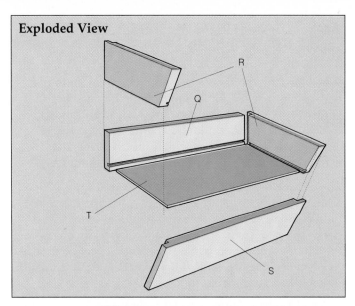

Top View

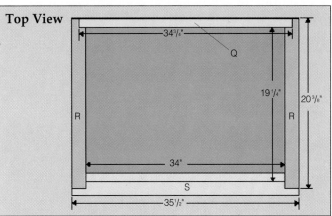

Back Layout

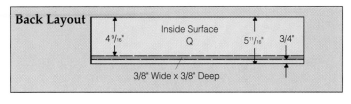

Side Layout

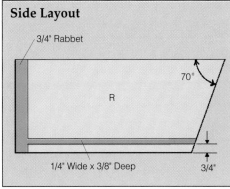

Front Layout

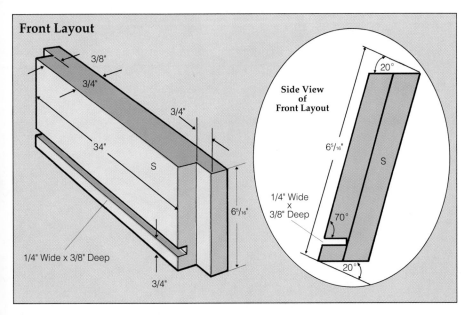

Child's Bed

When a child is old enough to graduate from a crib to a bed, he has reached a major milestone. This bed has the classic good looks of a captain's bed, and can be adapted to many other styles through variations on wood and colors. Two storage drawers underneath the bed hold extra linens or provide space for toys and clothing.

The bed itself is relatively easy to make and a desk attachment can be secured to one end. This unit can be built completely from hardwood plywood or a combination of plywood with solid lumber. If you choose to stain the wood, you will want to add veneer edge strips to provide a finished look. If the bed is to be painted, add wood filler to the edges.

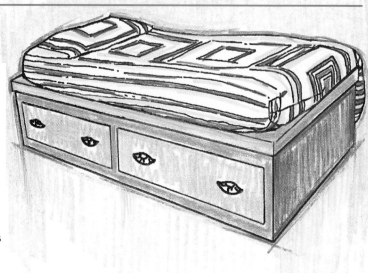

1. Machine the Dividers. All of these pieces are cut to size from plywood (see Top View). You can edge-glue the center divider from scraps left over from cutting the top and bottom. To help ventilate the mattress, drill about 20 (1") holes in the top of the unit.

Tools & Materials

Bed Frame

- [ ] A (1) 3/4" x 38⅞" x 74⅞" Hardwood Plywood (For the top)
- [ ] B (1) 3/4" x 37⅞" x 74¼" Hardwood Plywood (For the bottom)
- [ ] C (1) 3/4" x 11" x 37½" Hardwood Plywood (For the center divider)
- [ ] D (2) 3/4" x 13¾" x 38¼" (For the sides)
- [ ] E (1) 3/4" x 13¾" x 74¼" (For the back)
- [ ] F (4) 3/4" x 2" x 36" (For drawer spacers)
- [ ] G (2) 3/4" x 2" x 76½" (For the side top frame pieces)
- [ ] H (2) 3/4" x 2" x 39" (For the end top frame pieces)
- [ ] J (1) 3/4" x 2¾" x 75" (For top cross member)
- [ ] K (1) 3/4" x 2¾" x 75" (For bottom cross member)
- [ ] L (2 3/4" x 1½" x 13¾" (For outside vertical cross members)
- [ ] M (1) 3/4" x 2¼" x 13¾" (For center vertical cross member)
- [ ] N (2) 3/4" x 2¼" x 37½" (For feet)

Drawers: (Requires a table saw)

- [ ] P (2) 3/4" x 8⅛" x 34¾" (For fronts)
- [ ] Q (4) 3/4" x 2¼" x 36" (For sides)
- [ ] R (2) 3/4" 8" x 30¾" (For backs)
- [ ] S (2) 1/4" x 31¼" x 35⅜" (For bottoms)

Hardware:

- [ ] (2 Pair) Drawer Rollers
- [ ] (4) Drawer Pulls
- [ ] Nail Set
- [ ] Sanding Paper
- [ ] Sander
- [ ] Finish, Stain or Paint
- [ ] No. 8 x 1¼" Flathead Wood Screws
- [ ] Veneer Edging Tape (Optional)
- [ ] (4) Plate Casters
- [ ] 4d Finishing Nails
- [ ] Screw Plugs
- [ ] Wood Filler
- [ ] Carpenter's Square
- [ ] Mattress

2. Machine the Sides and Back. Unless you are using plywood, you may have to edge glue 3/4" stock to create boards of sufficient width from which to cut the sides. These pieces are machined to create one left and one right side, in a mirror image of each other (see Side Layout).

Each side is machined with one standard shelf dado and one standard flush-back rabbet (see Flush-Back Rabbet, page 27).

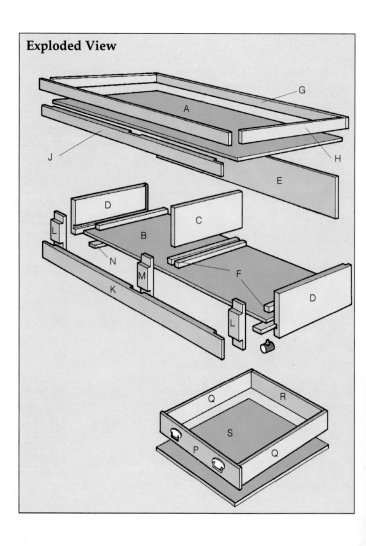

Exploded View

Top View

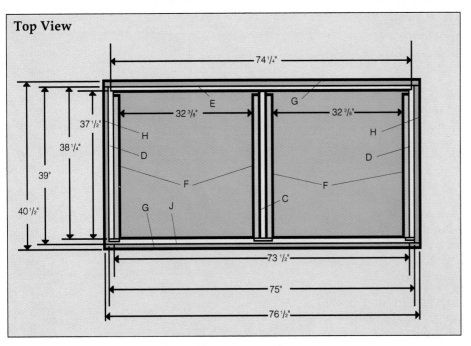

3. Machine the Spacers. Machine four pieces of 3/4" stock each 2" x 36", to serve as drawer spacers (F). These will support the drawer roller system.

4. Machine the Cross Members. The vertical cross members combined with the top and bottom cross members create a grille that holds the drawers in place. (The top outside frame pieces simply hold the mattress in position). Rout or dado the top and bottom cross members (see Top and Bottom Cross Member Layout) on the inside face, to accommodate the vertical cross members.

Rout or dado the vertical outside and center cross members (see Vertical Cross Member Layout) on the front face surface, as shown, so they will mate with the top and bottom cross members.

Side View

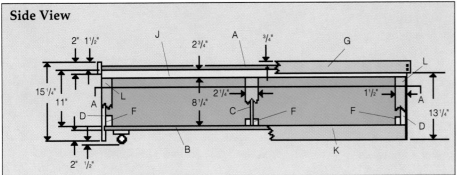

Side Layout

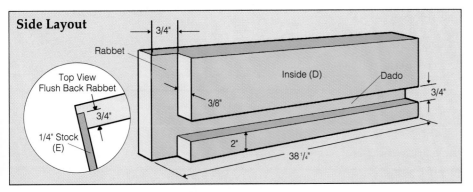

Vertical Cross Member Layout

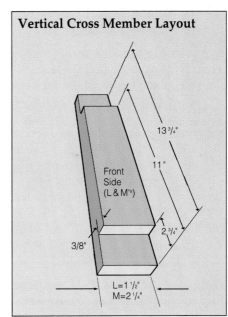

Top and Bottom Cross Member Layout

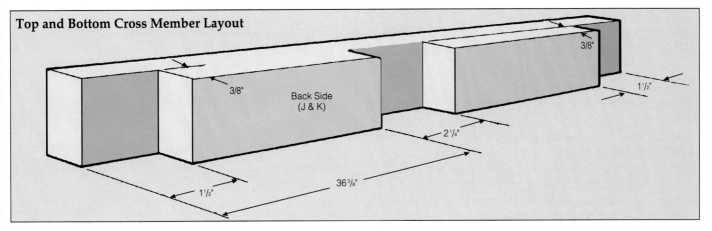

5. Machine the Drawer Pieces. The bed has two large drawers underneath which have flush fronts. Once constructed, rout the front edges of the two fronts with a 1/4" radius quarter-round router bit.

The dimensions of the sides and back may have to vary from the specifications on the materials list to conform to the hardware used to mount the drawers. Follow the hardware manufacturer's instructions for clearances and such, to determine actual final drawer size.

No matter what the size, the steps to create the drawers are the same. Make grooves 1/4" x 1/4", set 1/4" up from the bottom of the sides and back pieces with a dado cutter (see Drawer Back). Set the matching groove on the drawer front as indicated; this groove will be placed farther from the bottom edge of the piece because the front is wider than the sides and the back pieces (see Drawer Front).

Use a regular cutting blade on a table saw to make the additional cuts on the back of the drawer front. This is done in two steps. First, cut to a depth of 3/8" horizontally in from both the top and bottom edges of the front. Cut horizontally 1¹⁄₈" in from the sides. Then make vertical cuts to remove excess wood, adjusting blade height as required. Clamp the drawer front to a jig to cut the ends. It is too long to ride securely against the rip fence of the saw without support. Cut the drawer bottom from plywood. Cut the parts for both drawers at the same time.

6. Assemble the Drawers. To assemble a drawer, predrill for nails if wood is hard. Nails are used to attach the sides to the front and the back of the drawer. Create an immovable stop to hold the drawer parts fast while you nail them together. A piece of scrap wood tacked to the work surface is sufficient. Then put the drawer front face down on the work surface, flush up against the stop, and glue and nail one side in place. Glue and nail the sides to the front. Set the nails with a nail set. When the sides are secure, slip the drawer bottom into place in the 1/4" grooves in the sides and seat the bottom in the groove in the drawer front. Spread glue onto the ends of the drawer back. Lay the drawer on its side in order to nail through the drawer side into the back. Set these nails.

7. Square the Drawers. Turn the drawer upside down (bottom-side up) and use a carpenter's square to square it up. If it is out of square, grip opposite corners of the drawer and push and pull toward the middle until it is squared.

Drive nails or brads through each side of the bottom into the sides to lock the drawer in its proper squared shape.

8. Sand the Pieces. In all likelihood, the plywood will not need to be sanded. However, make sure that the top surface under the mattress is splinter-free so that it cannot harm either a child or the mattress. Rough- and finish-sand the sides and back on the outside face only. The four drawer spacers and all the various cross members need not be sanded until after they have been glued together during the assembly process. Rough- and finish-sand the top outside frame pieces on all edges and surfaces except the bottom edges. Sand the drawers as well.

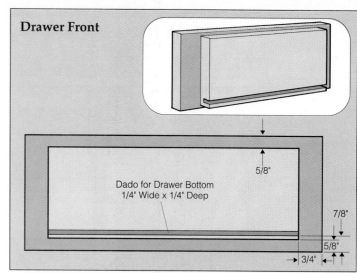

Drawer Front

Dado for Drawer Bottom
1/4" Wide x 1/4" Deep

5/8"

7/8"

5/8"

3/4"

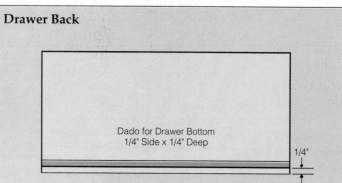

Drawer Back

Dado for Drawer Bottom
1/4" Side x 1/4" Deep

1/4"

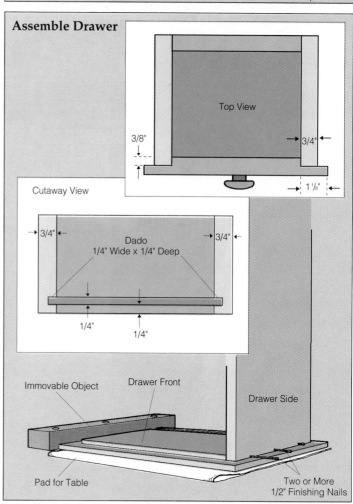

Assemble Drawer

Top View

3/8"

3/4"

1¹⁄₈"

Cutaway View

3/4"

3/4"

Dado
1/4" Wide x 1/4" Deep

1/4"

1/4"

Immovable Object

Drawer Front

Drawer Side

Pad for Table

Two or More
1/2" Finishing Nails

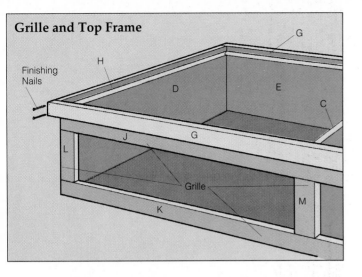

Grille and Top Frame

Finishing Nails

G
H
D
E
C
L
J
G
Grille
M
K

9. Assemble the Grille. Use glue to assemble the grille, the front framework through which the drawers will pass (see Grille and Top Frame). Check for square and then clamp. Recheck for square and adjust the clamps if necessary.

10. Assemble the Bottom, Sides and Back.
Install the bottom into the grooves on the sides with glue and 4d finishing nails. Clamp and check for square. Invert the unit and install the back. Glue the back to the sides and nail 4d finishing nails from the back into the sides. Secure the lower edge of the back with No. 8 x 10 1/4" flathead wood screws driven through the bottom into the lower edge of the back. Drill pilot holes, offsetting them slightly to avoid screwing into the same section of grain fibers. Turn the unit right side up.

11. Attach the Grille, Spacers and Dividers.
Attach the grille to the sides, bottom and top with glue and No. 8 x 1 1/4" flathead wood screws. Countersink all screws and fill the holes with wood putty or screw plugs.

Next, attach the top end frame pieces with No. 8 x 1 1/4" flathead wood screws, countersunk, driven through the sides into the frame. Clamp the frame to the side to hold it in place while driving in the screws. Complete the top outside frame by putting glue on the ends of the outside

frame pieces. Drive 4d finishing nails through the face of the front and back top frame pieces into the ends of the shorter outside frame pieces. Slide the divider into position and drive 4d finishing nails through the face of the front grille and back.

12. Install Drawer Channel-Roller Systems.
To ease drawer operation, a channel-type drawer-roller system should be installed. This type of roller system comes in a variety of lengths at 2" intervals and should be cut to the exact size with a hacksaw. Measure the depth of the bed frame from the front of the drawer brace to the back, less 1/4" and then the drawer-side length, less 1/4".

First attach channels to the left and right sides of the bed frame. Make sure the front end of each channel is flush with the leading edge of the drawer brace (see Drawer Channel-Roller System, left).

Then, attach the drawer channels to the drawer (see Drawer Channel-Roller System, middle). The roller plate at the back of the drawer should be flush with the bottom of the drawer. Now you are ready to insert the drawer into the side channels.

13. Complete the Bed. Invert the bed and install the feet and heavy casters near the bottom corners of the bed frame. Place the bed on the floor, and reaching through the top, install the drawers and finalize positioning of the spacers on which the hardware rests. Then drop the top into place on the bed. The top will support the mattress. It rests on the top edges of the sides and on the center divider but is not attached. If you have used plywood, glue veneer tape on all edges and sand. If the bed will be used without the desk addition, finish the unit with paint or stain of your choice. If the desk attachment is to be used, paint or stain when both components are completed.

Drawer Channel Roller System

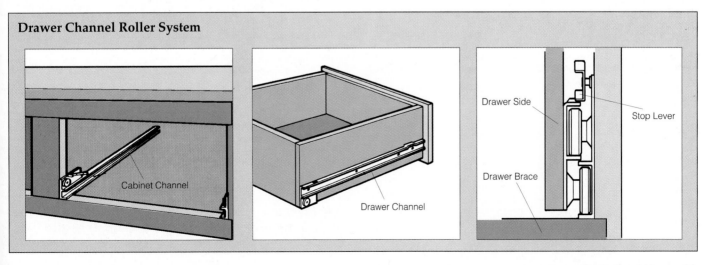

Cabinet Channel

Drawer Channel

Drawer Side

Stop Lever

Drawer Brace

Child's Bed Desk Attachment

The captain's bed lends itself to the addition of a desk at one end. This space-saving arrangement may be all that is needed for a youngster's early school years, when simple writing and hobby projects do not require an elaborate study area. Match the design of the desk attachment to that of the bed unit. You can do so through the selection of hardware for the drawer pulls and the style of the desk legs.

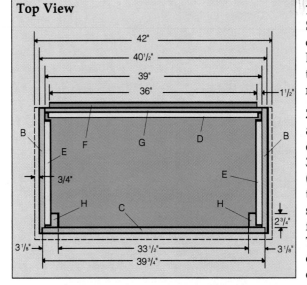

Tools & Materials

Desk:

- ☐ A (1) 3/4" x 18" x 42" (For top)
- ☐ B (2) 3/4" x 5 1/2" x 17 1/4" (For sides)
- ☐ C (1) 3/4" x 5 1/2" x 39 3/4" (For front)
- ☐ D (1) 3/4" x 1 1/8" x 36" (For top brace)
- ☐ E (2) 3/4" x 1 1/2" x 13" (For side top braces)
- ☐ F (1) 3/4" x 2 1/2" x 36" (For spacer)
- ☐ G (1) 3/4" x 29 1/4" x 39" (For desk back) Hardwood Plywood
- ☐ H (2) 2 3/4" Diameter x 28" (For turned legs)
- ☐ Router   ☐ Saber saw

Drawer Parts:

- ☐ J (1) 3/4" x 4" x 34 1/4" (For front)
- ☐ K (2) 3/4" x 3" x 15 1/2" (For sides)
- ☐ L (1) 3/4" x 3" x 31 7/8" (For back)
- ☐ M 1/4" x 14 7/8" x 31 1/4" (For bottom) Hardwood Plywood

Hardware:

- ☐ (2) Drawer Pulls
- ☐ 4d Finishing Nails
- ☐ 1" Brads
- ☐ Screw Plugs
- ☐ Monorail Drawer Slide
- ☐ Wood Veneer Tape Edging
- ☐ No. 10 x 2" Flathead Wood Screws
- ☐ No. 8 x 1 1/4" Flathead Wood Screws

Top View

42"
40 1/2"
39"
36"
1 1/2"
B B
F G D
E E
3/4"
H C H
3 1/8" 33 1/2" 3 1/8"
39 3/4"
2 3/4"

Side View

18"
17 1/4"
No. 8 x 1 1/4" Screws
A
B
3 3/4"
5 1/2"
G
H
No. 10 x 2" Screws; Countersink All Screws with 3/8" Diameter Plugs
29 1/4"
24 1/4"
30 1/2"
Bed
F
1/2"

Front View

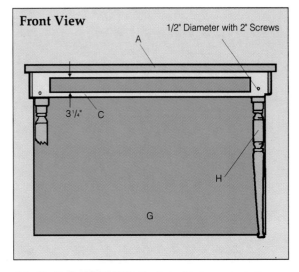

A
1/2" Diameter with 2" Screws
3 1/4" C
H
G

1. Machine Top and Sides.
Rout a 3/8" radius curve around all top edges. Dado sides (see Side Layout), to make left and right mirror image pieces.

2. Machine Front Piece and Desk Back.
The front drawer frame has a 3 1/4" x 33 1/2" cutout in the middle (see Front Layout). Create the cutout by drilling 1/2" starter holes in each of the four corners of the cutout. Then use a saber saw for cutting out the opening, connecting the starter holes.

3. Machine Drawer Parts.
The steps used to machine the drawer parts are the same as the steps for the bed drawers (see Machine the Drawer Pieces, page 32), except for the dimensions used (see Drawer Front, page 35).

4. Prepare the Legs.
Legs may be purchased premade or you may lathe the legs yourself.

5. Sand the Pieces.
Rough- and finish-sand the edges and upper surface of the top, along with the back edge and outside surfaces of the two sides and the outside face of the front. Rough-sand the edges of the cutout area of the front. Rough-sand the spacer on the two end edges, one long edge, and on one face. Top braces, desk back and turned legs need only fine sanding. Sand drawer parts as needed.

Side Layout

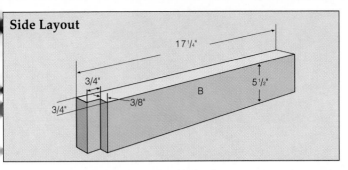

17 1/4"

3/4"

3/4"

3/8"

5 1/2"

B

Front Layout

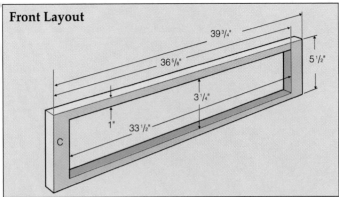

39 3/4"

36 5/8"

5 1/2"

3 1/4"

1"

33 1/2"

C

Drawer Front

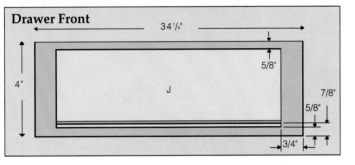

34 1/4"

4"

J

5/8"

7/8"

5/8"

3/4"

6. Assemble the Drawer. Place the drawer front face down on a padded surface and brace it securely (see Assemble Drawer, page 32). Glue and nail the sides to the front with 4d finishing nails and set nails. Slip the bottom into the drawer. Apply glue to the ends of the back. Place the drawer on its side and hammer 4d finishing nails through the sides into the back and set nails.

Turn the drawer upside down (bottom-side up) and check it for square with a carpenter's square. Drive 1" brads through the bottom into the sides (one on each side) to hold the drawer square while the glue dries. Once glue sets, fill nail holes neatly with wood filler so that additional sanding will not be necessary.

7. Assemble the Desk. Attach wood veneer tape to the two sides of the desk back. Attach the top brace to the plywood back with four No. 8 x 1 1/4" flathead screws. Predrill 3/8" diameter plug holes into each side and the front (see Front and Side Layout). Attach the two turned legs with No. 10 x 2" screws driven through the holes to anchor them securely. Install the two top braces onto the sides with No. 8 x 1 1/4" flathead wood screws. Attach the plywood desk back using No. 8 x 1 1/4" flathead wood screws. Cover these wood screws by gluing in screw plugs. Invert the desk and attach the top with No. 8 x 1/4" flathead wood screws through the top braces. Cover screws with screw plugs.

8. Install the Drawer and Roller System. First, read over the manufacturer's instructions. The following are general instructions for installing a monorail roller system.

Mark a vertical center line on the back of the drawer and attach the rear roller, centered on this line with the roller flange even with the bottom of the drawer back (see Attach Rear Roller). Screws for this attachment usually come as part of the roller system.

Attach the side rollers (see Attach Side Rollers) to either side of the drawer opening. Position these rollers so that they will contact the drawer sides, and keep the sides from rubbing on the front of the cabinet.

Cut the monorail to length 1/8" shorter than the distance from the back edge of the drawer brace to the back of the cabinet. Install the bracket to the back brace with wood screws. Insert the monorail in the bracket and attach the front of the monorail to the cutout in the front of the desk. The monorail must be level and it must be precisely centered in the drawer opening at both the front and back of the desk. Measure carefully and double-check before you attach these parts to the desk (see Attach Monorail).

To install the drawer, tilt it forward slightly and insert the rear roller in the monorail (see Install Drawer). When you feel the roller drop into place, bring the drawer back to level and slide it smoothly into the desk.

9. Attach and Finish the Desk. To attach the desk to the bed, screw the spacer onto the bed first, using No. 8 x 1 1/4" flathead wood screws. Then, screw the plywood desk back to the spacer. Stain or paint the desk and bed unit and attach all hardware.

Attach Rear Roller

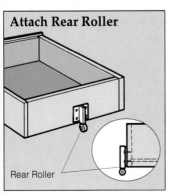

Rear Roller

Attach Side Rollers

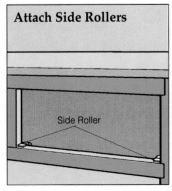

Side Roller

Attach Monorail

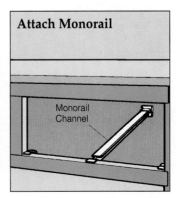

Monorail Channel

Install Drawer

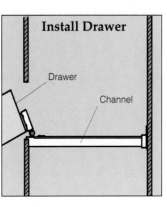

Drawer

Channel

Never-Ending Storage Needs

Aside from a place to sleep or study, almost all furniture in a kid's room is designed for some type of storage. The need for storage appears at an early age and lasts throughout childhood.

While individual pieces can help the problem, an overall plan is the best long-term storage solution. Since most kid's rooms are small, efficient use of space for storage is very important. Parents are the major users of storage in a nursery. Needs here are to accommodate clothing, changing and tending necessities, bedclothes, a few toys, and items such as playpens, strollers and the like.

Since a child's use of his room changes constantly as he grows, keep on top of his needs by assessing how the storage really works from time to time. As soon as possible, invite the child to spearhead the quest for space and ways of solving storage problems so he can put things away himself.

In shared rooms, make sure each child has his own storage areas, clearly demarked. Your storage provisions can mitigate many tussles, especially if the kids are like the odd couple, one neat and one messy.

Ingenious joining clips make units such as this built-in easy to assemble with lumber or shelving.

This colorful chest makes storing toys easy.

Overall storage principles apply to children's rooms as well as those of adults. Among these are:

■ Store what you need where you need it most. For instance, you want to keep sheets and blankets near the crib instead of across the room. A child will be more inclined to put away toys and tools for a hobby if stored near the work surface he uses where they can be easily stored and readily retrieved.

■ Make sure storage furniture works well. Some furniture is particularly designed for efficient storage, such as many changing tables. Open areas (instead of drawers) allow parents to readily reach for diapers, cleansing aids, talcs and the like without fumbling

A full wall of closets solves the storage problem neatly in this room. Wallcoverings and fabrics are used to dress it up.

Lowered rods that enable a child to put away his own clothes and wire baskets for toys aid him in developing a sense of order. Most units can be reconfigured for infinite variety.

Wicker baskets are always a good source of additional storage. Note, too, the special shelves that hold cherished toy collections in plain view.

around and being distracted from an active baby. You can adapt many existing units by carefully planning for your needs, and then retrofitting the unit and reorganizing the stored items in the most efficient ways.

■ Anticipate future needs. Purchase storage units that are flexible enough to grow with a child's expanding horizon. Adjustable shelves, furniture that can be reconfigured (such as stackable drawers and bookcases), and convertible closet storage units are good examples of versatile storage pieces that can change and grow with a child.

■ Involve the child in the planning and selection of storage units. She'll be more likely to use storage units for putting away things if she likes them. Some children like everything in its place and all out of sight, except for what is currently being used. Closed storage systems suit them best. Others like to have everything visible, finding the zany clutter stimulating and comforting. Open shelving units are best for these children.

■ Make closets work efficiently. A wide variety of closet storage units have been designed to make the most of precious space. In fact, by creating vertical storage that accommodates the very different needs of children, virtually double the amount of items can be stored. In early years, there's little need for hanging clothing; open shelves and drawer units are most efficient. When clothes that should be hung are part of a child's wardrobe, rods and shelves arranged to just clear the length make efficient use of space.

■ Let children store their belongings.
Clairson International, makers of
Closet Maid storage systems, has
compiled research that shows that
the goal of parenting a child to
become a self-reliant, responsible
adult is made easier with storage he
himself can utilize. Encouraging a
child to assume responsibility for
his own space will help him feel
self-reliant and develop positive self-
esteem, effortlessly teach good
organizational skills and cut down
on scolding and nagging him to
straighten up his room, the company
maintains. Easily managed wheeled
carts that can be stored in a closet or
pulled out to straighten up after play
enable children to clean up
themselves. Lower hanging rods
allow a child to hang up his own
jackets, as do delightful children's
clothes racks and trees designed at
lower levels.

■ Make putting away easy. Open
storage shelves can be used as early
as toddler years to hold favorite toys,
such as stuffed animals, within reach.
Baskets and boxes on shelves can
organize small objects and keep them
in place. Organize them by color
coding, cartoon signs, or words when
children are old enough to use them.
Kids can make the labels and help
create the storage arrangement that
best suits them, rearranging as their
needs change.

■ Avoid attractive nuisances. When
kids hit the climbing stage, make sure
that storage units, particularly
shelving, will not tip easily. Anchor
them to walls, floors or ceilings if
necessary. Equally important, keep
items a child wants within reach, not
engagingly in sight on a high shelf.
Attractive nuisances are those things
that while dangerous, are irresistible
to a child. You will want to eliminate
them from your storage plans.

This unusual storage-sleep-study center is reinforced with special interlocking hinges that make this unit safe for older children.

Castle towers transform storage closets built into this room. Lights in the windows atop the units act as night-lights, a charming detail in the design.

Stackable Portable Storage Drawers

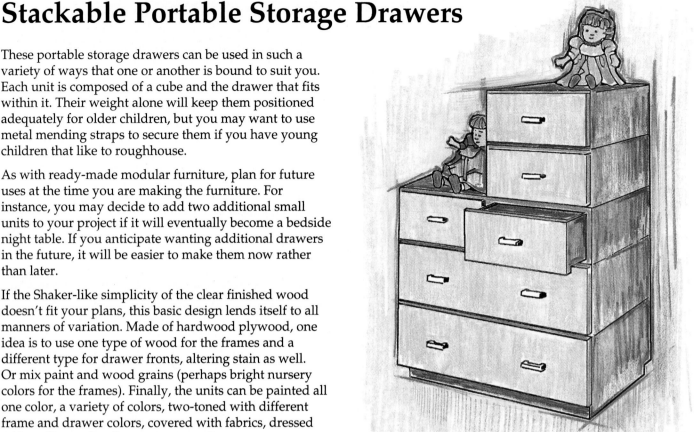

These portable storage drawers can be used in such a variety of ways that one or another is bound to suit you. Each unit is composed of a cube and the drawer that fits within it. Their weight alone will keep them positioned adequately for older children, but you may want to use metal mending straps to secure them if you have young children that like to roughhouse.

As with ready-made modular furniture, plan for future uses at the time you are making the furniture. For instance, you may decide to add two additional small units to your project if it will eventually become a bedside night table. If you anticipate wanting additional drawers in the future, it will be easier to make them now rather than later.

If the Shaker-like simplicity of the clear finished wood doesn't fit your plans, this basic design lends itself to all manners of variation. Made of hardwood plywood, one idea is to use one type of wood for the frames and a different type for drawer fronts, altering stain as well. Or mix paint and wood grains (perhaps bright nursery colors for the frames). Finally, the units can be painted all one color, a variety of colors, two-toned with different frame and drawer colors, covered with fabrics, dressed with wallpaper borders—you name it.

The successful completion of this project requires intermediate woodworking skills.

Tools & Materials (For 4 small drawer units and 2 large ones)

- ☐ (2) 3/4" x 4 'x 8' Hardwood Plywood
- ☐ (1) 1/8" x 4' x 4' Hardboard
- ☐ (1) Piece of 1" x 2" x 6' Lumber
- ☐ (1) Piece of 1" x 2" x 3' Lumber
- ☐ 60' Veneer Tape to Match Plywood (Optional)
- ☐ Metal Mending Straps (Optional)
- ☐ Steel Thumbtacks
- ☐ 8d (2½') Finishing Nails
- ☐ Carpenter's Glue
- ☐ Penetrating Resin Finish
- ☐ Circular Saw or Table Saw
- ☐ Wood Putty or Filler
- ☐ Drawer Pulls
- ☐ Brush (For applying finish)

1. Cut All Pieces. Use the saw to cut the 3/4" plywood into pieces according to the diagram for four small and two large drawer units. Plan the best direction of wood grain for both box sides and drawer fronts. Vertical grain on sides, horizontal grain on fronts is a pleasing pattern.

2. Assemble Cubes. Use butt or miter joints, allowing an extra inch on all sides to be mitered. Set the blade to 45 degrees and cut miters if you are not butt-joining.

To butt cubes, rough-sand pieces. Butt side panels onto cube tops and cube bottom edges. Attach with glue and finishing nails, making sure the cube is square. Clamp while glue sets. Cut hardboard backs and nail and glue to rear of cubes.

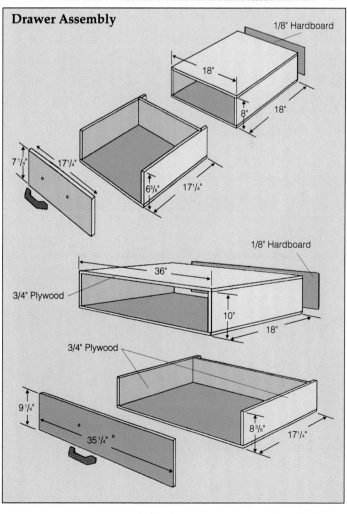

Drawer Assembly

1/8" Hardboard
18"
18"
8"
7¼"
17¼"
6³⁄₈"
17¼"

1/8" Hardboard
3/4" Plywood
36"
10"
18"

3/4" Plywood
9¼"
35¼"
8³⁄₈"
17¼"

3. Assemble Storage Drawers.
Rough-sand all surfaces except edges. Predrill drawer fronts for hardware but do not attach. Butt sides to bottom and to back panel (see Drawer Assembly, page 39) making sure the unit is square. Glue and nail.

Set the drawer front face down on a padded surface. Toenail the sides to the front, centering the drawer part on the back of the front panel.

4. Tape Edges. Add veneer tape to all exposed edges; allow to dry.

5. Make a Platform Base. Cut 1" x 2" lumber to form a rectangular base, 34" long front and back and 16" long on each side. If metering, allow an extra inch on all sides. To butt platform base, follow directions above for cubes. Set side pieces inside front and back pieces. Attach with glue and finishing nails, making sure the base is square. Clamp while the glue sets. Finish edges with veneer tape, and sand all surfaces.

Attach the base to the bottom cube with toenailed finishing nails and glue.

6. Finish the Surface. Finish-sand all surfaces not previously finished. Apply finish and allow to dry. Attach drawer pulls. Drive thumbtacks into drawer bottoms along sides to provide easier sliding into cubes. Stack cubes in whatever configuration is desired. For added stability, connect the cabinets with mending straps on each side of the back, screwing straps into the back edges of the sides.

Project courtesy of Georgia-Pacific Corp.

Tips for Working with Hardwood Plywood

■ Hardwood plywood commonly comes in 4'x8' sheets either 3/4", 1/2" or 1/4" thick and is designed for inside use only.

■ Stack panels face-to-face and store in a clean, well-ventilated area away from direct sunlight and excessive heat or moisture. Maintain relative humidity at approximately 50 percent at 70° F. Cover to keep panels clean.

■ Handle panels carefully to prevent damage to corners and edges.

■ Good measurements are essential. Remember: Measure twice, cut once. When mitered edges are involved, measurements include an extra inch.

■ Always use a sharp blade when cutting to prevent splintering. When using a table, radial arm or hand saw, keep the panel's good side face UP. If using a portable circular saw, keep the best face DOWN (see drawing).

■ To prevent splintering when using a dado blade or router, start by scribing the line you want to cut with a razor blade or utility knife.

■ The plywood is strong but the face is thin. When sanding, be careful not to sand through the face veneer. Orbital sanders are easier to control than belt sanders.

■ The best adhesives used with hardwood plywood include carpenter's glue, epoxies and hot melt (from glue guns).

■ Nails and screws work well in most situations, but when screwing into a panel edge use thin shank, drywall screws.

■ To conceal nails, set nail heads below the surface and fill the hole with matching wood putty and sand smooth. To conceal screw heads, first counter-bore 3/8" diameter holes, then cover the hole with hardwood plugs.

■ Finish edges with hardwood lumber strips, iron-on edge tape, ready-made molding or paperback veneer tape, available at home centers. Be sure tape is firmly attached so that a child cannot pull it off. Another alternative is to finish edges (after filling with wood filler) by either painting or staining.

■ Use a sealer initially when using a dark stain to avoid a blotchy appearance. Test a small sample piece before applying final finish to be sure you will like the effect.

■ To apply a finish, sand, brush with a small broom, then wipe with a tack cloth. Apply one coat of oil or water-based stain if desired. Allow the stain to dry completely then sand with 4/0 (000) steel wool; wipe again with a tack cloth. Apply two coats of finish (cabinet varnish or polyurethane). A satin or semi-gloss finish is beautiful for wood grains. Allow to dry between coats, sand with steel wool, and wipe with tack cloth. Apply a final coat of paste wax for a mellow sheen.

Stacking Bookcases

Open shelving is ideal furniture for a children's room. Used initially for toys, the same units (even with added interlocking elements) can be used later for hobby supplies, books, tapes or video games. These handsome interlocking pieces are simple to build lend themselves to a variety of looks. Although a four shelf unit bookcase is shown, building 12 units from two sheets of plywood is more economical.

Tools & Materials (For 3 bookcases, each with 4 shelves)

☐ (2) 3/4" x 4' x 8' Hardwood Plywood (Good both sides)

    A (12) 3/4" x 11⁵/₈" x 31" Cut from Plywood (For shelves)

    B (24) 3/4" x 12" x 11⁵/₈" Cut from Plywood (For end panels)

☐ C (9) 1" x 6" x 34" Lumber (For backing boards)

☐ D (3) 1" x 4" x 34" Lumber (For top backing boards)

☐ Veneer Edge Tape (Optional)

☐ No.8 x 1½" Flathead Wood Screws

☐ White or Yellow Wood Glue

☐ Router or Dado Blade for Table Saw

☐ (At least 4) 14-Tooth Jigsaw Blades

☐ Circular Saw or Table Saw   ☐ Wood Filler

☐ Sandpaper   ☐ Jigsaw

☐ Palm Sander   ☐ #000 Steel Wool

☐ Screwdriver   ☐ Drill

☐ 2"x3" Paint Brush   ☐ Paint or Stain

1. Cut All Pieces. Cut two 4' x 8' plywood panels to create shelves (A) and end panels (B). Cut 1" x 6" lumber for backing boards (C) and 1" x 4" lumber for top backing boards (D). If you choose to stack fewer or more shelving units you will have to adjust the number of backing boards and top backing boards needed.

2. Cut End Panels. Make slot cuts in the end pieces 3/4" x 2³/₄" and set in 1" from the edge. Cut a 3/4"-wide groove 3/8" deep and 2³/₄" up from the bottom of each end piece, 12 on one side, 12 on the other side as mirror images (for left and right sides of shelves). Be sure veneer is running in the same direction on all end pieces.

3. Round End Panel Corners. Mark the corners of each piece by measuring in 1" from the edge of each side. Use a compass to draw the arc and cut with a jigsaw.

4. Sand All Pieces. Use wood filler where necessary.

5. Assemble the Shelves. Begin assembly by countersinking three holes for No. 8 x 1½" wood screws at each shelf edge on the end panels, set in and center 1" from the sides. Lightly coat shelf ends with wood glue and insert into the groves. Draw tightly with wood screws and allow the glue to dry. (You may want to fill the screw holes if you plan to paint the units.)

6. Finish the Edges. Cover front edges with veneer tape. Allow to dry, and fill with wood filler if painting.

7. Paint or Stain. Paint or stain units individually, including backing boards; allow to dry.

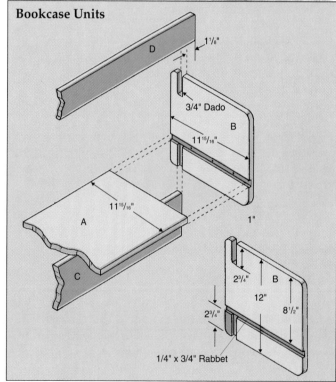

Bookcase Units

8. Assemble the Unit. Place first unit on the floor. Slip a 1" x 6" backing board into the back groove on top. Fit the next shelf onto this backing board, and repeat up to the top shelf, which is finished with a 1" x 4" board.

With back pieces in place the units stack easily and provide good stability up to about 6' (depending upon loads). For greater stability, run a #6 x 2" wallboard screw into the back of each end piece 1" below the top and bottom, to secure the back board.

Courtesy of Georgia-Pacific Corp.

Early American Bookcase

This pleasantly chunky bookcase, measuring 36"x 36"x11", is scaled nicely for a youngster, since she can easily reach every shelf before she's very old. Line up more than one of these along a wall, and use square baskets to hold small items. Larger toys fit right in. Match the bookcase to other traditionally styled furnishings by using the same wood and stains.

A change of the shaping on the bottom foot and elimination of scalloping on the top can create any style for this bookcase. For a more unique touch, paint decorations, such as climbing vines over a pickled country stained finish, along the sides and top of the bookcase. In addition, when a child starts collecting treasures, consider adding a light strip behind the top scallop (extend the wiring through the back). What child wouldn't be thrilled to see favorite dolls, soldiers, cars or seashore treasures spotlighted; a night-light built around his best dreams.

Tools & Materials

- [ ] A (1) 3/4" x 11" x 36" (For top)
- [ ] B (3) 3/4" x 10" x 33³/₄" (For shelves)
- [ ] C (2) 3/4" x 10¹/₄" x 35¹/₄" (For sides)
- [ ] D (1) 3/4" x 3¹/₂" x 34¹/₂" (For front foot)
- [ ] E (1) 3/4" x 1¹/₈" x 33" (For top back brace)
- [ ] F (1) 3/4" x 2" x 33" (For top scallop)
- [ ] G (1) 1/4" x 32¹/₂" x 33³/₄" (For back)
- [ ] (6) Bar Clamps, Strap Clamps
- [ ] Router
- [ ] Wood Glue
- [ ] Stain or Paint
- [ ] Wood Filler
- [ ] Saber Saw or Band Saw
- [ ] Sanding Paper
- [ ] Nail Set
- [ ] Circular Saw

Hardware:
- [ ] No. 8 x 3/4" Flathead Wood Screws
- [ ] No. 8 x 1¹/₄" Flathead Wood Screws
- [ ] No. 8 x 1¹/₂" Flathead Wood Screws
- [ ] 4d Finishing Nails
- [ ] 3/4" Brads

1. Machine the Top. The top should be a single board if possible, especially if you plan to make the bookcase from pine. Cut it to the dimensions given and round the side and front edges, top and bottom, with a 3/8" quarter-round router bit.

2. Machine the Back. The back can be made of 1/4" plywood, and is best if it matches the remaining wood of the unit. If the bookcase is to be painted, then a less expensive plywood such as fir can be used. Birch and pine are very compatible woods in accepting stains, so birch can be used for the back of a pine bookcase. Cut it to the dimensions given.

3. Machine the Sides. Cut the two sides. You can leave the bottom plain (a flush cut) or create an Early American cutout (see Scalloped Foot, page 28). You can match these

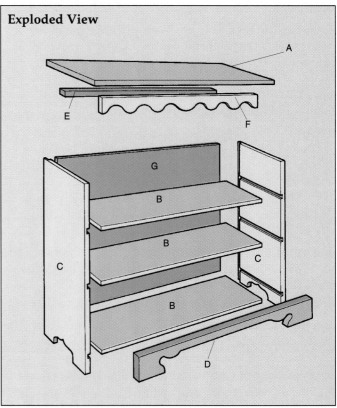

Exploded View

furniture pieces or create a design entirely of your own, perhaps to match other furniture you plan to acquire. Cut standard shelf grooves and standard back grooves in the sides (see Side Layout, page 43), so that they are a mirror-image pair.

4. Cut the Top Scallop. Cut part F to size and choose one of the suggested scallop patterns (see Scallop Variations or create your own). Copy and transfer it to the piece. Cut out the pattern with a saber or band saw.

5. Machine the Front Foot. The dimension given for the front foot is 1/16" wider than the bookcase so that you can sand it flush after installation. If you wish, round the leading edge with a 3/8" quarter-round router bit. Cut out a foot pattern or leave the foot flush for a modern look.

6. Sand the Pieces. Rough- and finish-sand the upper surface, the two ends and the front edge of the top. The remainder of the top should be rough-sanded. Rough-sand the front face of the top scallop, the scalloped edge and the back side of the scallop. Then, finish-sand the front face of the top scallop. Rough- and finish-sand the shelves' top surfaces and rough-sand the bottom surfaces, but don't sand the front edges yet.

Rough- and finish-sand both surfaces of the side pieces. Sand the top edge of the front foot. Rough-sand the front and downward edge of the back brace.

7. Assemble Sides and Shelves. Spread glue on the grooves and on the ends of shelves. Work the glue into the end fibers and fit the shelves into the grooves. Check for square and clamp above each shelf. Use six bar clamps, three on the front and three on the back, to hold the shelves firmly until the glue has set. Use 4d finishing nails to nail from the underside of each shelf into the sides. Set the nails with a nail set. Check again for square. Use clamps to pull into square if necessary.

8. Add the Scallop and Back Brace. While the clamps are in place, apply glue to the ends of the top scallop and the back brace. Fit the back brace into place first, set flush with the back groove. Nail through the sides into the ends of the top scallop and back brace with 4d finishing nails. Set the nails with a nail set. Clamp the scallop and brace to assure that the glue will set (strap clamps will work).

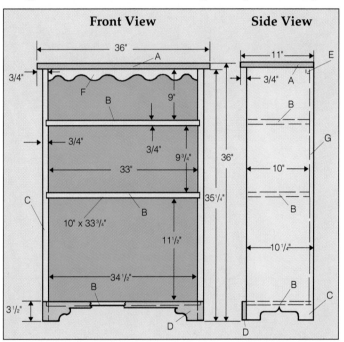

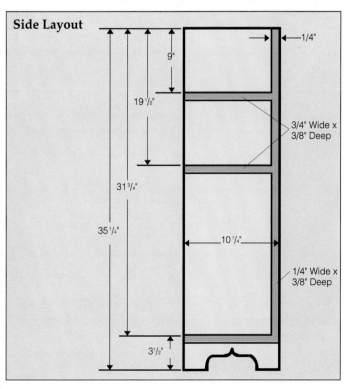

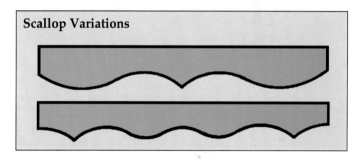

Scallop Variations

9. Add the Front Foot. Place glue on the leading edge of the sides and the bottom shelf before placing the front foot into position. With 4d finishing nails, nail through the front foot into the leading edges of the sides and shelf. Clamp until set.

10. Add the Top. Place the top upside down on a padded surface and invert the bookcase onto the top. The back edge of the top should be flush with the back edges of the sides. Drill three countersunk pilot holes each through the top scallop and the back brace. Drive No. 8 x $1^3/_4$" wood screws through the pilot holes into the top. Fill the screw holes with colored wood filler. Allow to dry.

11. Finish the Unit. Once assembled, the front edges of shelves and the front foot should be sanded flush. Finish and polish all pieces, including the back which has not been attached. (It will be much easier to finish the bookcase without the back in place.)

12. Add the Back. Fit the back into position and fasten it to the sides and shelves with 3/4" brads. The upper edge of the back fits flush against the top back brace. Use four No. 8 x 3/4" flathead wood screws, evenly spaced, to secure the back to the brace to provide added stability.

Toy Chest

A simple box with a lid, especially one on wheels, can serve as a toy chest, a place to perch, or can be put to use for any number of playroom activities. You can make a toy chest any size you wish, following the general format of this chest. Or, use this traditionally shaped and sized toy chest. Not just any old box will do for a toy chest. An extremely important safety feature for all toy chests is some kind of support for the lid. While you can use hand tools to create this entire chest, it will take moderate woodworking skills.

Tools & Materials

- ☐ A (2) 3/4" x 14" x 19½" Glued-Up Stock (For sides)
- ☐ B (2) 3/4" x 14" x 30" Glued-Up Stock (For front and back)
- ☐ C (1) 3/4" x 18" x 28½" Plywood (For bottom)
- ☐ D (1) 3/4" x 20½" x 31" Glued-Up Stock (For top)
- ☐ E (2) Cross Braces 1" x 3" x 18"
- ☐ F (4) Corner Blocks 1" x 1" x 12¾"
- ☐ (4) Flat-Bottomed Casters with Screws
- ☐ (2) Blanket Hinges with Screws
- ☐ (2) Spring-Loaded Lid Supports
- ☐ No.8 x 1¼" and No.8 x 1½" Flathead Wood Screws
- ☐ Sander or Sanding Block, Sandpaper
- ☐ Stain, Paint or Clear Finish
- ☐ Handsaw, Table Saw or Radial Saw

☐ Glue	☐ No.8 Finishing Nails
☐ Wood Filler	☐ Arm Saw
☐ Hand Drill or Power Drill	☐ Doweling Jig
☐ 1⅜" Spiral Dowels	☐ Bar Clamps
☐ Screwdriver	☐ Hammer

NOTE: You may choose to use 3/4" hardwood plywood as a substitute for the glued-up stock. If so, cover edges with veneer tape. Use wood filler if you intend to paint the box. You also may find ready-made precut glued-up stock at home center stores.

1. Dowel the Top and Sides. If you decide to alter the dimensions of this chest, be sure that the opposite sides are exactly the same size. When the box is assembled, measure its inside dimensions for fitting the bottom and the outside dimensions for fitting the lid. Then you can glue and dowel the stock to make the sides and lid. Lay out pieces of 3/4" stock, alternating the direction of the grain in every other piece to minimize warpage. Smooth the butted edges of the stock with a jointer (or hand plane) until the pieces fit perfectly against each other. Mark four parallel lines across the width of the pieces (at a right angle to the butted edges) so that they divide the stock into five equal parts. Use a doweling jig to drill a 1"-deep hole at the four marks in each facing edge.

Squeeze glue into the holes along the edge of one piece of stock and drive in 1⅜" spiral dowels; glue along the facing edge of the next piece and drive it onto the dowels.

Exploded View

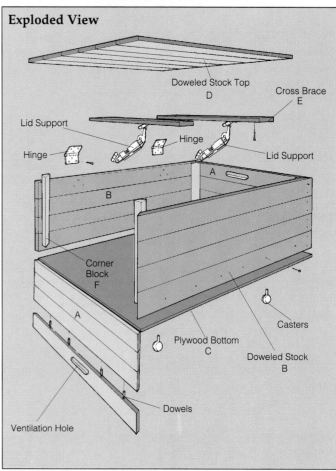

Repeat the procedure until you have glued and doweled all the stock for the piece you are making. Fix the stock in a bar clamp and tighten the clamp until the glue squeezes out of the joint lines. Wipe the glue away with a warm, damp cloth. Allow the stock to dry overnight.

Use the same procedure for making the other sides and lid (or use plywood or ready-made glued-up stock as mentioned).

2. Cut the Sides and Assemble the Box. Once pieces are dry, cut each side to the proper size and miter each end at 45 degrees. Cut out ventilation holes which double as handles. Use glue and No. 8 finishing nails set below the surface or countersink No. 8 x 1½" wood screws to attach the sides. Check to see that the box is squared as you assemble the pieces.

3. Cut and Fit the Corner Blocks and Bottom. Cut the bottom from 3/4" plywood to the inside dimensions of the box you are building. Rip corner blocks to 45-degrees, shorter if necessary to make them 1¼" shorter than the depth of the box, and miter the tops at 45 degrees. Install them with glue.

To attach the bottom, apply glue on all four sides of the bottom, then turn the box on its side to position the bottom 3/4" up from the bottom of the sides and secure with No. 8 x 1½" wood screws driven in through the sides.

4. Assemble the Lid. Cut the glued stock for the lid to 1" larger than the outside dimensions of the toy chest. Cut the cross braces to about 2" shorter than the inside width of the box; they must clear the edges for the lid to close. Attach the braces across the lid with countersunk No. 8 x 1¼" flathead wood screws. Rout a 3/8" radius curve on the entire lid edge.

Note: Adequate ventilation must be provided should a child become trapped inside the box. Create a ventilation gap in one of the following ways: Add 3/8"-high blocks at the four corners of the unit; extend corner blocks to this height beyond the sides; or add corner blocks to the lid.

The Consumer Products Safety Commission (CPSC) recommends that all toy chests have the following safety features:

Lid support. Hinges should be used in conjunction with a support that holds the lid open in any position in which it is placed. A spring-loaded lid support that will not require periodic adjustment is recommended by the CPSC for use on toy chests. This protects fingers as well as heads from a falling lid.

Ventilation. Two methods of providing ventilation are to drill ventilation holes that will not be blocked if the chest is placed against the wall. Holes on all sides would solve this problem. Another alternative is to set the lid of the chest high enough to provide a gap all around the top.

Locks & Latches. Do not, under any circumstances, put a lock or latch on any chest including this toy chest. Having covered the safety features, feel free to decorate the chest as uniquely as you wish.

5. Finish the Chest. Position the lid so that it overlaps the edges on all sides by the same distance. Attach it with standard blanket chest hinges and the spring-loaded brace lid supports, which you can find in hardware stores and home centers. Fill in screw and nail holes with wood filler. Attach flat-bottomed casters to the bottom of the box at the corners. Glue veneer tape on the outer edge of the lid if using plywood. Finish the toy chest any way you wish.

6. Finish the Toy Chest. Dates, names, decals, stencils, themes of a child's favorite pastimes and plain geometric shapes are all decorative possibilities. A treasure box with a nautical theme might enchant a child who's enamored with the sea. Ballet shoes with intertwining laces might catch the fancy of a budding dancer. Plain wood grains are always nice, and paint to match the rest of the room is less fanciful but may suit your scheme best.

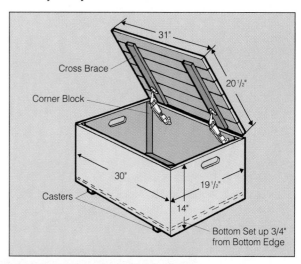

A clear finish allows the beauty of the wood to show on any chest, even an unfinished, ready-made piece.

A darker stain on wood letters makes an ideal decoration.

Big-Rig Toy Box

Here's a pull toy that can hold favorite possessions and make a game of cleaning up. Imagine an entire fleet of these stashed in their own "garage" at the base of a closet or along a wall, each with its own color scheme. You can even model the trucks after trucks your child might see on the road—a favorite department store label, telephone repair truck, United Parcel Service, garbage truck, fuel, moving vans—anything that takes your fancy. Or, put an outline of the item to be stored in the truck on the side, decorating one with blocks, another with a teddy bear, a third with a ball, you name it. Scrap shelving can be used to construct this truck if you have it on hand.

Tools & Materials

- ☐ A (2) 3/4" x 11" x 29" Any Stock or Hardwood Plywood (For sides)
- ☐ B (2) 3/4" x 11" x 8½" Any Stock or Hardwood Plywood (For back and front)
- ☐ C (1) 3/4" x 8½" x 22½" Any Stock or Plywood (For bottom)
- ☐ D (1) 1/2" x 5" x 10" Any Stock (For cab front)
- ☐ E (1) 1/2" x 3½" x 10" Any Stock (For cab top)
- ☐ F (2) 1/2" x 1/2" x 3" Scrap (For window rails)
- ☐ G (1) 1/4" x 1/2" x 10" Scrap (For bumper)
- ☐ (2) 1/4" to 3/8"x1/2" Dowel (For headlights)
- ☐ (3) 3/4" x 1" x 10" Any Solid Stock (For axles)
- ☐ (6) 3/4" x 4" Any Stock (For wheels or purchase wheels)
- ☐ Fly Cutter or Wood Lathe (For turning wheels if needed)
- ☐ (6) No. 8 x 1¼" Roundhead Wood Screws
- ☐ No. 4 and No. 6 Finishing Nails
- ☐ Screw Eye and Rope Pull Handle
- ☐ (12) Washers
- ☐ Wood Putty
- ☐ Band Saw, Saber Saw
- ☐ Screwdriver
- ☐ Glue
- ☐ Paint
- ☐ Sander and Sandpaper
- ☐ Hammer

1. Cut and Assemble the Box.
Mark the shape of the two side pieces on 3/4" plywood or scrap 1" x 12", according to dimensions given (see Box Layout). Cut pieces with a band saw, saber saw or coping saw. Cut the front and back ends of the trailer and bottom piece to the given dimensions. Sand the pieces thoroughly.

Attach the back and front end pieces between the sides (see Side View) with glue and No. 6 finishing nails countersunk below the surface. Attach the bottom inside the box so that the bottom is flush with the bottom edges.
Use No. 6 finishing nails countersunk below the surface. Fill nail holes with wood putty, let set and sand smooth.

2. Add the Cab.
Cut the cab front to the given dimensions, sand it

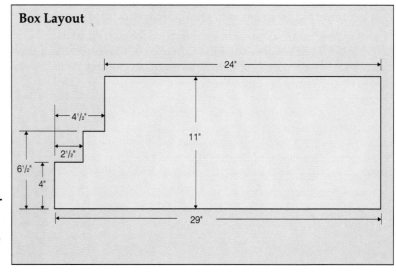

Box Layout

24"
11"
4½"
2½"
6½"
4"
29"

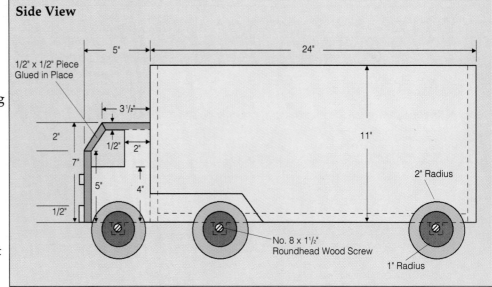

Side View

5"
24"
1/2" x 1/2" Piece Glued in Place
3½"
2"
1/2"
2"
7"
11"
5"
4"
2" Radius
1/2"
No. 8 x 1½" Roundhead Wood Screw
2" Radius
1" Radius

and attach to the front flush with the edges and bottom of the truck body. Glue the truck front edges, then nail on the front with No. 6 finishing nails set below the surface. Cut the cab top to size, sand it, and install it on the top of the cab, butted against the trailer end. Glue the top edge of the truck body and back edge of cab top, position and countersink No. 6 finishing nails.

Hold a piece of 1/2" x 1/2" scrap against the side of the cab where the window rails should be positioned (see Side View, page 46) and mark the angles at the bottom and top. Cut the two as marked, sand them lightly, and install with glue and No. 6 nails, allow to dry.

Cut the front bumper from a piece of 1/4" scrap (or 1/8" hardboard scrap) and glue it in place at the bottom of the cab front. Cut slices from 1/2" dowel for the headlights, position them on the front and glue into place.

Note: It is easier to paint these decorative trims before gluing them on.

3. Attach Axles and Wheels. Cut the axles to given dimensions from 3/4" stock, sand the axles and attach them to the bottom of the box and cab (see Side View, page 46) with glue and No. 4 finishing nails. Allow the glue to dry. Cut the wheels on a band saw, fly cutter or lathe to the given size and sand smooth, paying attention to the rims to make sure the wheels will roll smoothly. Or, purchase wheels at a home center, hobby or hardware store. When the wheels are done and the truck is dry, sand it all over then paint it. You can block off areas with tape to combine colors in geometric designs and stripes on the truck body.

When the wheels are dry, drill a hole through the center of each wheel one size larger than the No. 8 roundhead screws. Attach the wheels to the axles with No. 8 x 1 1/4" roundhead wood screws and a washer on either side of each wheel to the axles on the truck. Don't screw in the wheels all the way in; instead leave enough room for them to rotate easily.

To attach a pull-rope, screw a screw eye into the front of the truck on the back side of the cab at the bottom.

Exploded View

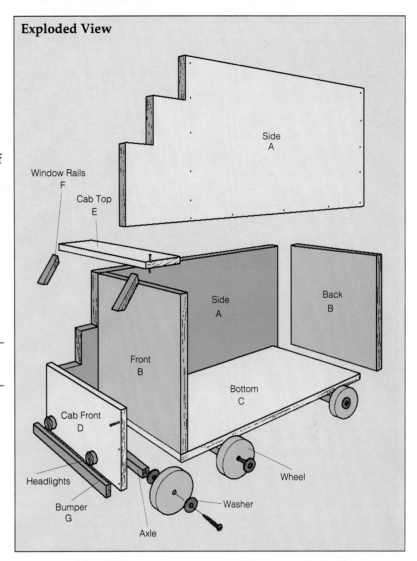

Front View

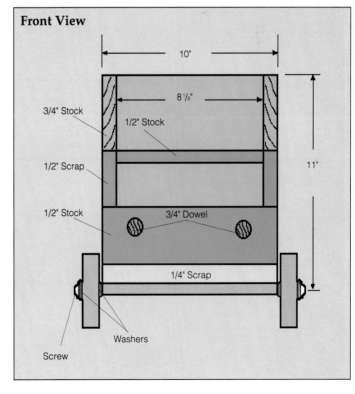

Personality Decorating

K ids are equipped with personalities from the minute they're born. Some are fussy, some are calm; some are interested in everything; some are born dreamers. While parents solely select the furnishings for a nursery, from that point on, the child's personality and preferences should take an increasing role in his room's decoration. The real trick is to make sure that you understand your child's wishes, and that they can be dovetailed with your own wants and needs.

The decorative elements that make up the personality of a room include the colors and textures used; the treatment of the floors, walls and ceilings; window decorations, bed linens and lighting, as well as furniture style. As you will discover, the possibilities for any child's room are enormously vast.

Far and away, the elements that have the most impact upon a room are color and texture. The color wheel is a helpful and important instrument and we will show you how to use it to your advantage. It helps to have a broad imagination when it comes to using color and texture. The combinations are infinite.

While Mickey and Minnie Mouse star in the soft and punchy pastel color scheme in wallcoverings based on a seaside theme (above), deeply saturated blue and red combine with crisp white in the snappy color scheme found in the photo far left.

Color is the Key

Color preferences are highly personal, and in many cases, pretty inflexible. With virtually an entire spectrum from which to choose, you can develop a color scheme that's totally your own and as fanciful as you wish. Before you begin, there are some basic principles worth considering that may serve as guidelines for both adult and children's spaces. These include different kinds of color schemes, using color to disguise and to glamourize, methods of altering color schemes, using colors to harmonize with a room's basic character, and ways of selecting color schemes with your child. Also included are some quick (and relatively inexpensive) ways of creating colorful kid's rooms.

Types of Colors

The perception of warmth and the perception of coolness are the first basic divisions for colors. Warm colors have attributes of liveliness and happiness, and are ideal selections for rooms that are on the north or eastern exposures where outside light is cool. Dreary rooms benefit most from warm colors. Ruddy reds, tantalizing oranges and sunny yellows in all their variations are members of this group. Cool colors are soothing and restful, and can diffuse the glare of hot southern or western exposures flooding into a room. Blues, greens and neutrals are cool.

Hue often is used interchangeably with color. It refers to the various points on the spectrum—the parts of the rainbow as distinguished from the other parts. It includes the primary colors and all the variations in between. For instance, blueberry, purple, grape, plum, magenta, and mulberry are just a few hues between blue and red.

Saturation refers to the amount of intense pure color used to make up a color. For instance, the red of the United States flag is fully saturated as red, while the same color takes on the look of a watermelon pink when diluted with white. A luscious ruby's deep jewel tone results from red's dilution and deepening with the addition of black.

Tints refer to colors that have had white added to them, such as the difference between royal blue and baby blue, or red and pink. Shades describe colors that are closer to black in value. The ultimate light tint value is white; the ultimate dark shade is black. All colors in their infinite variety can be changed along this range of values.

A kid with a crayon box develops a sense of color differences, without realizing what she's learned. It's easiest to develop color schemes, which involve the pleasant combining of colors, with a basic understanding of how colors interact. The color wheel was invented by scientists to show how colors relate to one another. Interior designers use the wheel to develop workable color schemes.

Know Your Colors

An artist's color wheel is composed basically of 12 colors, divided into primary colors, secondary colors and tertiary colors. Colors that fall between the basic hues listed on the wheel are called complex colors, because they are made up of sophisticated mixes of basic pigments and hues.

A good place to start is to see where colors fit on the wheel and to study how they are positioned in relation to each other. This is the departure point for developing color schemes.

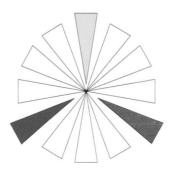

Primary Colors. While the psychological "primary" colors are red, yellow, blue and green, the true triad of primaries are yellow, red and blue. These are known as "primaries" because you cannot create them by combining any other colors. Additionally, all colors are composed of parts of these colors. Green does not qualify as a primary because it is composed of yellow and blue.

Fully intense red, yellow and blue are balanced for high energy in this wallcovering with a border.

Secondary Colors. Orange, purple and green are the secondary colors. They are composed of equal parts of the primary colors. Orange is made up of equal parts of yellow and red; purple is made from equal parts of red and blue; and green results from equal parts of blue and yellow.

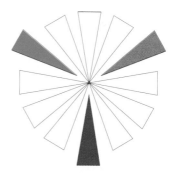

Tertiary Colors. Also known as intermediary colors, this group is created by mixing equal parts of a primary color and its closest secondary color. Tertiary colors include yellow-orange, red-orange, red-purple, blue-purple, blue-green and yellow-green. You may know them by their home furnishing names. Put in decorative terms, yellow-orange becomes an apricot hue, red-orange becomes a terra cotta when darkened with grey, red-purple becomes a mulberry in a dark tone or dusty rose in a light tint, blue-purple becomes a lavender with the addition of white, blue-green becomes turquoise or a teal hue, and yellow-green becomes a celedon or chartreuse.

Wood tones are generally composed of orange hues to which either grey or black have been added. Since most rooms include wood tones, in furniture, flooring or molding, you should include them as you develop your scheme.

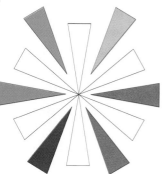

The secondary colors, green, orange and purple, are rendered in this lovely room in soft tones of sage, peach and lavender.

Neutral colors include the greys, whites, dull browns and blacks that do not add hues to a scheme. They provide a background, the necessary relief, upon which a color scheme can be played. Even greys that are colored with warmth (such as pickled, white-washed wood tones, putty colors or beiges) are neutral enough to act as background players in any color scheme.

Sesame Street characters on a brilliant border wide enough to cover most of the lower wall are rendered in pure yellow-orange, blue-green and touches of purple in the wallcovering.

Select the Dominant Color

Most children's rooms will need to undergo a gradual shift in color scheme as the inhabitant gets older. While nursery schemes are totally in the providence of the parents, children at the toddler stage can show preferences for colors, which may or may not change as the child grows older. Once a child develops a need to express her own dominance over their realm, usually by mid-elementary school age, she will want to help decide on the scheme. And preteens are notorious for using their rooms and their color schemes as a means of expression.

In selecting colors for nurseries, optometrists will tell you that babies distinguish shapes and contrast most clearly. Black and white contrasts are much more interesting to a newborn baby, since she may miss the nuances of subtle contrasts until her eyes develop more fully. Sharply defined colors are easier to distinguish for a crib-age baby and bright, primary colors are far easier for a baby to see than the soft pastels often used to decorate a nursery.

The fact that a child distinguishes contrasts and primary colors first does not have to determine your selection of a color scheme. Bright colors and contrasts can always be added to a nursery through toys, crib bed linens, and even a child's clothes. Furthermore, an overly enthusiastic baby may need the calming effect of a soothing color scheme more than the intellectual stimulation of a room totally designed around sight development. The bottom line is to use the colors in the nursery that you like the best. The dominant color, if it is a neutral, can serve as the departure point for any scheme you might want to develop. Many designers therefore recommend either white, beige, putty or grey walls and floor coverings for a neutral platform upon which to build.

In selecting a distinct color, a most versatile plan is to use a light, white-infused tint of your color choice. For instance, a pale yellow will be less intrusive than a bright curry color. The same yellow can support a scheme of palest pastels now and also work with deeply saturated colors at a later time.

While you probably know what your color preferences are, you'll have to do some detective work with most children to determine their likes and dislikes. Here are some ways to figure out your child's likely choices, even if she doesn't know them herself.

■ Look over a child's drawings and see if she almost always selects one color over others in drawings where color makes no difference. (She may literally use green and brown for trees but what colors does she use to color a rainbow, bird or butterfly wings when the choice is entirely up to her?)

■ Have her select favorite colored blocks and organize them by preference. You can do the same with pickup sticks, gum drops, or any other multicolored resource you have in your home.

■ Color schemes are highly individual and sophisticated in many children's picture books. Leaf through picture books and put adhesive paper markers on pages a child particularly loves, then look to see if a color preference pattern emerges.

■ Examine her wardrobe. Most children select clothing based upon color preference. Take that as a color clue.

■ Most towel displays in large stores include a variety of colors suitable for walls. See which colors attract your child.

■ A loved quilt, poster, painting, rug, comforter set, or piece of painted furniture can spark an entire color scheme.

Combine Colors into Schemes

Schemes are developed by combining colors, using their relationship to one another on the color wheel as a guide. Once you've decided on a basic color you can develop an outstanding scheme around it.

Monochromatic Schemes. These are the easiest to develop, since only one color is used and variations are created by adding texture, patterns and shapes. Usually restful, monochromatic schemes include totally pink rooms, totally blue rooms, or totally neutral rooms.

Monochromatic schemes, especially based on beiges or greys, lend themselves to infusions of color through accents. With the addition of new accents, you can easily alter a monochromatic scheme to freshen it up as years go by.

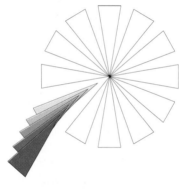

Variations in texture and pattern keep this monochromatic color scheme exciting.

Analogous or Related Schemes.

Side-by-side neighbors on the color wheel are used to develop these schemes. They are one of the easiest schemes to do well, since there is little tension from one color to another and the effects are invariably pleasing. For instance, you might select a very pale true blue as a primary color and select pale seafoam blue-green and forest green for accent colors.

Variation in value, intensity and texture add interest to these schemes. Popular analogous schemes include fuschia and violet combinations for little girl's rooms.

Contrasting Schemes.
These schemes are developed by using one color and accenting it with its exact opposite on the color wheel—its contrasting color. Equal amounts of both colors create conflicting tensions, while dominance of one helps settle the scheme down. Variations in tint and hue often bring these schemes to life. For instance, a red and green combination might be too intense, while a predominantly pink scheme with dark green accents would be as stunning as blush peonies blooming among foliage in the spring. Consider, too, the classic good looks of blue and white to offset a room where lots of wood furniture (a derivation of an orange hue) dominates.

Triadic Schemes.
The synergy of three hues equidistant on the color wheel makes these schemes time-honored winners. Often used with traditional furnishings (such as a patriotic scheme of red, white and blue with brass or gold accents), these schemes have many variations. Countless nurseries are wonderfully decorated through schemes of palest pink, blue and yellow. True primaries of red, blue and yellow often dominate preschooler's rooms, where manufacturers have used the colors in everything from stuffed toys to storage bins.

Neon colors take their cutting edge from triadic schemes that combine purple, orange and lime green, often with accents of white and black.

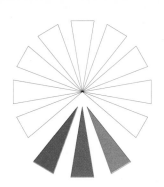

This shared room has been decorated with an analogous color scheme using a blended mixture of fuchsia, violet and blueberry.

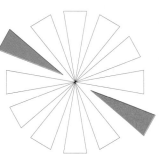

Pink and green always creates a winning contrasting scheme, as demonstrated in this young lady's room.

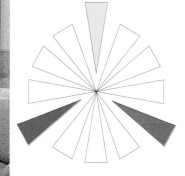

A perennial favorite for nurseries, pastel triadic schemes of blue, pink and yellow often are used. Notice how effectively the scheme is used in this baby's room.

Split- & Double-Contrasting Schemes.

Split-contrasting schemes consist of one hue combined with the hues on either side of the contrasting color. This kind of scheme is easy to assemble in ways pleasing to the eye. For instance, a ship-shape color scheme inspired by nautical flags might include sky blue walls with brilliant golden and tomato-colored accents. More exciting than a simple blue scheme with orange accents, a scheme like this suits a room that faces south. Cool colors dominate, but need to be perked up with warm, inviting additions.

Double-contrasting schemes, as you would assume, oppose two adjacent hues with their contrasting color. The four colors create a spirited combination with lots of zest and verve. The closeness of the neighboring colors on either side create a harmony that would be impossible without a similar close kinship.

While there are no hard and fast rules about organizing color schemes, by following some of the plans listed

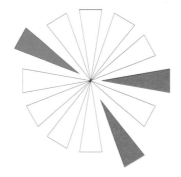

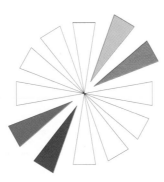

above you can be assured that the outcome will most certainly be a success. Possibilities are almost endless, a reality that often creates a problem when it comes to developing a starting point.

Color Scheme Proportions

Once you have chosen a dominant color, the next step is to decide how much of that color to use and where to use it. A good rule of thumb is to use the color on two-thirds of the room. The largest areas are made up of the walls and floor. Dominant colors often are best used when diluted, either with the addition of grey to mute the hue or with lots of white to lighten it.

Whichever type of scheme you select, you can place accent colors to fill up the remainder of the room. Examine your inspirational source (be it a rug or quilt), and pull out the colors that complement both that design element and the dominant color.

Consider some of the architectural implications of your selection of color and where it is placed. For instance, you can make a small room seem larger by selecting a cool color scheme. Keep the wall colors a lighter tint than that which you finally want, since close walls reflecting the color from one to another will intensify the color. For the same reason leave the ceiling white.

The exact reverse is true to make a room seem cozier. Select warm colors and swathe the walls, floors and ceiling in the same color, which multiplies a color's impact.

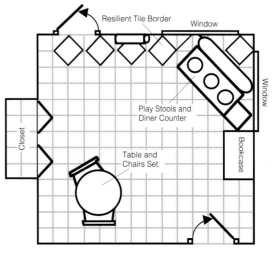

Intense colors of red, orange, blue and green joyously meld in this highly unique playroom. Solid colored vinyl tiles are used to pick up and echo the colors. Note the diamond patterned border which outlines the room.

Quick Tricks for Color-Schemers

Here are some quick, easy-to-do suggestions for incorporating color in a child's room.

■ Use wallpaper borders or paper just one wall to give texture and added color to a room.

■ Select a theme that inspires a color scheme. For example, the colors of a rainbow, nautical colors, flower beds, kites, a rustic log cabin, cartoon or movie themes, crayon colors, or a bed linen design.

■ Use your child's art as a source.

■ Change a scheme without changing the dominant color for a quick decorative pick-me-up. For instance, change a complimentary scheme of dominant pink with accents of greens into a triadic scheme with accents in sky blue and buttercup yellow. Or use the same pink and develop an analogous scheme by replacing the greens with plush purples, lavenders and peaches.

■ Vary textures to create more color excitement. For instance, a blue that is boring all in one texture can be enriched when used in high sheen window blinds, a matte finish on walls, a corduroy or homespun fabric on beds and perhaps a plush throw to take hard edges off a chair.

■ Be creative with paint, the less expensive remodeling tool. Use different hues on different walls.

■ Add a stencil pattern around doors and windows to create a wainscot at a child's eye level. Use professionally designed stencils from magazine articles, books or craft stores or try creating your own.

■ Take a motif from fabric you are using. For instance, match the teddy bear pattern on a coverlet by painting bears to match in the same colors as a motif on the walls.

The wonder of childhood is such that you can be highly original in your thinking and selections. Discussing and pinpointing a child's color preferences and then adapting them to his own room is one of the most private and personalized steps a child has in controlling his environment.

Self-Adhesive Deco

You can create a colorful, reuseable wall mural with jumbo room stick-ups. These decorations are made out of a durable, non-toxic substance which self-sticks to any smooth surface. The great thing about each set is that your child can enjoy the company of his favorite cartoon characters and when he grows out of them, or simply grows tired of them, they can be easily removed. Each set includes 10 pieces for you and your child to arrange any way you like (stick-ups shown are from Priss Prints).

Start with the Floor

Consider the floor treatment before undertaking anything else, even if you've selected a border pattern or an heirloom quilt as the pivotal inspiration for the room. Furnishings most often are neutral when it comes to selecting color schemes, textures and patterns. Conversely, the floor is second only to walls in the area it covers, and therefore has the potential for much decorative impact. With the great variety of wallcoverings and paints available for the walls, it's easier to choose a flooring first and to adjust the wall coloring to fit.

There are positive attributes to almost any flooring you might want to put into a child's room. Wall-to-wall carpeting provides a soft tactile sound-muffling surface where children may lounge. Wood flooring requires a minimum of upkeep, resists wear, and can be used as a giant worktable. Resilient flooring provides an easy-care surface at less cost than the installation of wood flooring. Ceramic tile outlasts almost any other flooring surface. Area rugs make up for the hardness of flooring surfaces and are inexpensive solutions for dressing a wood floor. Before you decide on which flooring you want, consider these pointers.

■ Get samples to take home, and view them on the floor in both daylight and nighttime lighting.

■ Take along swatches and samples of the other elements of your color scheme; don't trust your memory.

■ You may find that you fall in love with a different color rug than planned. That's fine as long as it goes with your color scheme.

■ Consider longevity and costs of replacement for each type of flooring, then compare costs per square foot including installation.

■ When measuring, don't forget the interiors of closets and any protrusions such as bay windows.

■ If you plan to move invest in area rugs.

Wall-to-wall carpeting is ready and waiting to become a plush playground in this girl's room.

Carpeting

In the long run, carpeting is a practical selection for children's rooms. Often, remnants can be inexpensive solutions to the smaller-sized rooms. These can be installed wall to wall or cut to fit as a room-sized area rug with bound edges.

Assuming the color's right, consider the texture next. A tightly woven or short pile surface withstands wear and tracking better than plush pile. However, feel is important since the rug will be a seating surface as well. Compare the fiber density by bending the carpet and seeing how much of the backing is exposed. You generally get what you pay for— the more dense the surface the more expensive the carpet. Salesmen will tell you if the carpeting has any warranty, or how long you can expect a carpet to last under normal wear.

Combinations of fibers and finishes have produced a generation of carpets that resist traffic and stains. It is preferable to purchase carpeting with built-in soil and wear resistance than carpeting to which a finish has been applied. Read warranties to be sure of the protections provided.

Padding is particularly important in a child's room. Even a tight weave carpet can feel luxurious with proper padding. Never lay carpet directly on the floor. The padding protects the backing and helps deaden sound.

In figuring carpeting cost , determine its laying pattern. Carpeting usually comes in 12'-wide rolls and is sold by length. If your room is 11' wide by 9', you'll use 3 yards (9') of the 4 yard (12') width, or 12 square yards. Multiply this by 9 to arrive at the cost per foot for comparison purposes.

Area Rugs

In using area rugs, consider the furniture placement in the room. Generally, furniture looks best when it is positioned totally on the rug or off of it. A table half on and half off a rug not only makes the room look unplanned, it's less efficient. Along the same lines, make sure rugs do not impede the movement of chairs. When area rugs are placed on a slippery floor, it is utterly essential that non-skid backing be used. In some cases a good solution is to attach Velcro tabs to the floor or use adhesive backing on the rug.

Floor Cloths

Consider a temporary protection of carpets for the more messy activities. A heavy-duty waterproof tarpaulin can provide the needed protection and is easily stored. Many are colorful enough as is; however, they can be decorated with fabric paint as well.

A more traditional variation of the tarpaulin is a canvas floor cloth, an Early American solution to the cost and scarcity of actual rugs. Decorate a ready-made straw or sisal mat for a modern-day variation on this theme.

Wood

Wood flooring, whether plank or parquet tile, is a good choice for a child's room since it is easy to clean and maintain. If you have old wood floors, they can be transformed easily by simply sanding and refinishing. If you want to change the look of a wood floor, consider the options. Most floors can be refinished with clear finishes, allowing the light wood to show through. For lighter looks, consider pickling, white-wash or tint treatments. Floors also can be painted and many can be stenciled with overall patterns or borders.

Resilient Flooring

Self-stick tiles are easily applied solutions, as are vinyl tiles and resilient sheet goods. Vary tiles for a fresh design. Resilient sheet can be combined with inset borders for variety. The non-splintering and easy maintenance advantages particularly suits a child's room. A nonskid surface texture is worth considering for a fledgling toddler.

Ceramic Tile

Because of its nongiving qualities, tile is an inappropriate surface if you think your children will be rough-housing in their rooms. Use area rugs to provide some cushioning. Tile takes all manner of abuse without losing its good looks. Impervious to water, it is an ideal surface for craft areas. Be sure the tile you choose provides a nonskid surface.

Updated colors in wool braided rugs make them perfect accessories for children's rooms.

Large open areas such as this expanse of flooring in a playroom become far more congenial when visually divided. Used on the floor here are parquet squares with feature strips in lighter finish, designed for use by a do-it-yourselfer.

Install Wall-to-Wall Carpeting

Before ordering carpeting, prepare a scale drawing on graph paper. Mark all doors, alcoves, obstacles and other unique room features. Prepare the subfloor by repairing damaged or loose boards. Remove the shoe molding from baseboards and discard. You will need to rent from your carpet dealer a seaming iron, a knee-kicker, a power stretcher and a carpet trimmer.

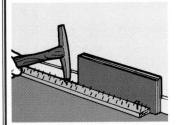

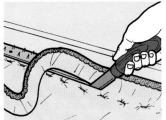

Install Tackless Strips. Cut strips with heavy-duty shears and nail them down a distance from the wall equal to two thirds the thickness of the carpet, with the tacks facing the walls. Use a spacer to place the strips evenly.

Fit the Pad. Cut the pad so it covers the entire floor. Butt pieces evenly at seams. If it has a waffle pattern, that side goes up. Staple the padding at 6" intervals around the room perimeter and anywhere it might slip.

Trim the Pad. Use a sharp utility knife along the inside of the tackless strip, leaving a 1/8" to 1/4" gap. Tilt the knife slightly away from the wall (creating a beveled edge) to prevent the pad from climbing.

Make a Rough Cut. Allow an extra 3" at room perimeter and seams. Cut loop-pile carpet from the front and cut-pile from the back. Notch edges, make a chalk line between notches and cut with a carpet knife.

Seam the Carpet. To cut a seam, overlap one carpet piece about 1" over the other. Use the top piece as a guide to cut the bottom piece. Butt tightly the two pieces. Insert a length of hot-melt seaming tape halfway under one piece. Make sure the adhesive side is up and the center is aligned with the carpet edge. Warm a seaming iron to 250° F, hold back one carpet edge, slip the iron under the other edge, hold for 30 seconds and then slide it slowly along the tape while you press both halves of the carpet down behind it onto the heated adhesive. Go slowly and be sure the two edges are butting. If not, pull them together and place a heavy object on them until they have time to bond to the tape. Let the seam set.

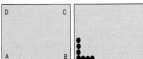

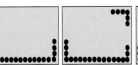

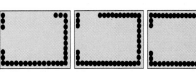

Stretch and Hook the Carpet. Walk around the room and shift the carpet so it lies smoothly. Trim the edge to overlap tackless-strip by 1" or 2". You will use three techniques: hooking (with knee-kicker), stretching (with power stretcher), and rolling (pressing carpet edge onto the strip nails). Place knee-kicker about 1" from the tackless strip, and at slight angle to wall. Bump it with your knee so it moves the carpet and hooks it on the strip. Pull the carpet taut with the power stretcher, using minimum of force so it does not tear. Check to make sure it is evenly stretched. If the seams or pattern are distorted, unhook and restretch. Follow the sequence above: 1) Designate corners A, B, C, D. 2) Hook corner A. 3) Stretch toward B. 4) Roll edge A-B. 5) Stretch toward C and hook. 6) Roll edge A-C. 7) Stretch toward D and hook. 8) Hook edge C-D. 9) Stretch toward edge B-D and hook.

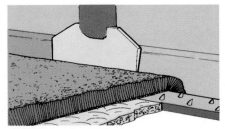

Finish the Job. Trim the carpet using a rented wall trimmer, adjusted to the carpet thickness. Slice downward at a 45-degree angle. Make cuts in corners and around obstacles with a utility knife. Leave just enough edging to tuck down into the gap between the strip and the wall. Push the edge of the carpet into the gap with a putty knife. If the edge bunches up, trim it a bit. The final step is to attach binder bars (standard metal edging) in doorways where the carpeting ends without a wall. Situate bars directly under the door. Trim the carpet so it will fit under the bar and tuck it in under the metal lip. Then, with a block of wood and a hammer, gently tap the lip down over the carpet edge so that it holds firmly.

Even a simple stencil, such as this leafy vine pattern, is enough to brighten up an otherwise plain floor.

Stencil a Floor

This traditional process involves applying paint through a mask. Commercially manufactured stencils are available at many craft shops, or you can create your own. Designs range from simple to intricate. An intricate stencil pattern may combine as many as 12 masks to achieve the final result. If you have never tried stenciling before, we suggest a simple, one- or two-mask pattern.

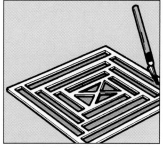

Cut the Stencil. Sketch a design on paper to see how well it holds together. Use a soft pencil to fill in the pattern, then transfer the pattern to a piece of acetate or waxed cardboard (look for stencil board at craft shops and art supply stores). Cut out the stencil mask with a sharp knife. Cut several exact duplicates of all your stencils so that you do not have to wait for one stencil pattern to dry before moving the mask to apply another pattern.

Apply Paint. The quick-drying lacquer paints are the best for stencils, because they do not spread under the edges of the stencil. Mark the location of the design on the floor. Tape the stencil in place. Special brushes with stubby bristles are used for stenciling. Dip your brush in the paint and touch a piece of paper to remove excess. Move the brush straight up and down, not back and forth, to fill in the stencil. Apply the paint lightly and go over the stencil several times.

Drying Time. Do not remove the stencil until the paint is dry. Then remove the tape and lift the stencil straight up. If any paint accumulates on the edges of the stencil or underside be sure to clean it off.

If you feel that the flat color of the stenciled pattern is not attractive enough, use a fine brush to add details to the design.

Finishing Coat. It is essential that you apply a final finish (polyurethane) to the floor to protect the stencil pattern from scratches and wear. You will need up to five coats of either a gloss or satin finish.

Walls & Ceilings to Celebrate

Walls take up the most visual space in a room. For this reason, you may want to treat them as neutral backdrops for the rest of the room. Or, you may want to create an entire fantasy wall treatment, affording your child hours of pleasure in looking at an enriching pattern or mind-expanding mural.

With walls as the palette, there are a number of different media to employ. These include paint, paint and borders (wallcovering and stenciled), wallcoverings, fabrics, paneling and special wall products such as molding.

Paint Walls Pretty

Paint offers so much to commend. After all, it's the least expensive wall treatment, it offers infinite color selections, it is relatively easy to change, and requires no special talents to apply. Wear and tear on a child's room can be overcome with a fresh coat or in some instances, with touch-ups.

One clever idea is to visually set off the lower section of the wall, which is most likely to need repainting before upper walls. A chair rail molding or border can separate the lower and upper wall, as can use of two different colors or tones. Consider painting the lower part of the wall if it has become soiled and leave the remainder of the wall untouched.

Children like to have walls brought down to size through such use of horizontal lines. Cavernous ceilings become cozier when the walls are divided horizontally. You can visually drop the ceiling by bringing the ceiling color down on the side walls, or by adding a visual border at plate rail height, in addition to chair height.

Stenciling is an extremely popular variation for children's room walls, adding both a cohesive decorating element and charming individualism.

This playroom, which brings nature indoors, includes many little animals on a wonderful wall mural, their animal tracks painted on the sisal rug.

Glossing it Over. Paints come in four basic degrees of gloss, each with its own special advantages. Flat paints hide surface imperfections most, but stain most easily. These are good choices for ceilings. Eggshell or low-luster paints resist stains more than flat paints and have a more lustrous appearance. Use these for children's room walls. Semigloss paints are more stain-resistant than flat paints and are an excellent choice where some glossy reflection is not a problem. The same paint can be used for walls, doors, woodwork and trim. High gloss paint is the least staining paint, often selected for woodwork and doors. It is easiest of all types to wash, but its high gloss reveals all wall imperfections.

Preparation. Any paint job works best with good preparation. This includes making sure the walls are clean, that any cracks are repaired, and all repairs are primed (so that they absorb the paint at the same rate

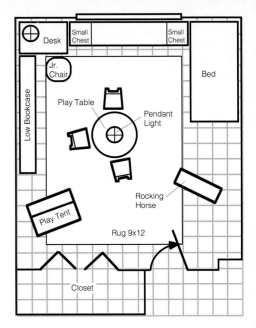

as the rest of the wall). The room should be set up with protection of what needs covering, and ample space to move ladders and equipment as necessary. In addition, it is particularly important in homes that are not new that all rooms, but especially children's rooms, are tested for lead paint for safety sake. If it is found, it must be removed before any new paint is added. Kids will mouth anything, including paint chips from old walls, a major source of lead poisoning, which can lead to brain damage in children.

It is equally important that you do not create airborne lead dust in sanding and scraping to prepare a room. Local cooperative extensions and government housing agencies can give you the most up-to-date methods of removing the dangerous lead. Evolving technologies and professionals who specialize in lead removal can be accessed through the Yellow Pages.

Here are some special tricks in making the painting job go more easily or creatively:

■ Punch holes in the rim of the paint can. Paint that normally collects there will run back into the can itself.

■ Use plastic wrap to keep brushes and rollers from drying during short breaks, such as for lunch or while stencil patterns set; when storing for longer periods, put them in an airtight storage, such as sealed plastic bags.

■ Since you don't want to create lap marks, you will want to paint from the dry, unpainted wall into the wet, painted wall section. A general

Wonderful heraldry designs were hand painted on this child's walls. The room is decorated with a Knights of the Round Table theme.

herringbone overlapping painting pattern working across and down the wall creates a uniform paint job.

■ If you are unsure of a color, buy a small sample and try it. Take advantage also of the new color-mixing computerized systems to select your colors, and paint a color sample (such as on a stir stick) which

you clearly identify by manufacturer and color for future reference.

■ Investigate the numerous painting techniques that can be used to decorate walls, such as rag-rolling, sponging, stippling, or spattering. You may even wish to create your own mural.

Get Ready to Paint

A room ready to paint will look something like the one shown here—use the picture as a visual checklist of basic preparations. The walls have been cleaned, slick spots roughened with sandpaper and old paint has been scraped and patched. The floor and any contents of the room that cannot be removed are completely covered. Switch and outlet face plates are removed from the wall, but are left in the room. Wall and ceiling light fixtures are either removed or loosened from wall or ceiling to be enclosed in plastic bags. Other hardware such as door knobs, picture hooks, and thermostat covers have been removed.

The order in which you should paint an entire room is as follows: 1) ceiling, 2) walls, 3) trim, 4) doors, and 5) windows.

If you are painting a surface that has never been painted before, you must first prime it. There are both latex and alkyd primers, but new wallboard (and wallboard patches) must be primed with latex.

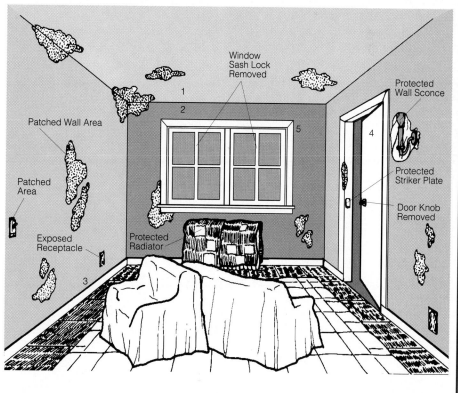

What little boy or girl would not want to launch himself into this graphic retreat? Bold colors and a bold design create an unforgettable abode.

Paint Blocks and Stripes. If stencil effects are not your style, consider using strips of paint to demark areas. Paint one area first and let it dry, then carefully tape off below a demarcation line with masking tape, covering the rest of the newly painted walls. Paint up to the taped line, making sure that your brush is not overly loaded with paint when you approach the line. Allow the paint of the new color to dry thoroughly before removing the masking tape.

A clear demarcation can be created easily with the use of wood molding. An inexpensive method is to cover over where two colors join with 1" lattice or molding. The molding can be painted in one of the wall colors or even a contrasting color for added punch. Paint the molding first, then apply it to the wall and touch up where needed (molding can be applied with either adhesive or molding brads).

Use a Roller

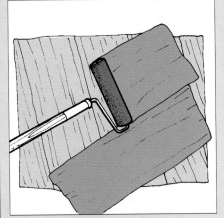

Spread the Paint. Roll the roller through the bottom of the paint pan, where the paint should not be more than 1/2" thick, distributing paint evenly over entire roller. Start laying paint on the wall in a zigzag. Go back over the zigzag with parallel strokes at a 90-degree angle.

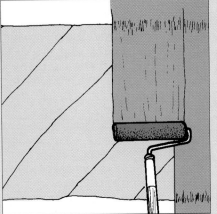

Finish the Paint. Without reloading the roller, finish this area by carefully rolling up and down, overlapping the strokes slightly, or side to side, if you have decided to do your finish strokes that way. Start and stop your strokes gently so as not to leave roller marks on the wall.

Stenciling Technique. Craft stores often stock ready-made stencil patterns you can use, but you may prefer to design your own. Quick-drying lacquer paints, applied over a clean dry surface, are most successful. They often are sold in small amounts at craft stores. Special brushes with stubby bristles are made especially for stenciling. Once you've selected a stencil, practice using it before applying it to the wall. Prime and paint a shelf or other accessory piece for practice, then incorporate the project into the room itself.

Acetate stencils are easier to use than those made out of waxed cardboard, but both work well. The stencil section goes from one repeated motif to another. The first step is to do a layout, based upon the height of your walls and the length. Using graph paper, make a plan of each wall, showing where the windows, doors, walls and any other architectural features appear. Then, mark the height where you want to put the stencil border. Plan where the stencil will repeat most effectively.

For example, if the border is a bow and ribbon design, you may want to center a bow over a window, or make sure that the bows are not lapped into the corners. Measure the distance between the centers of the major motifs in a stencil pattern and translate that onto your grid paper layout. Adjust it as necessary. You may find that the repeat of the stencil looks best when you do not use the entire stencil segment at the corner; use 1/2 of the segment or whatever suits the layout.

Usually, the stencil will have to be pieced where it meets itself after it encircles the room. Plan this juncture where it will be least conspicuous. Often this will be at the corner nearest the door to the room.

Handle the Paint

Prepare the Can. Use a hammer and nail to tap holes through the rim of the paint can to prevent paint from accumulating.

Load the Paint. Don't dip the brush more than half way up the bristles. Tap it lightly on the rim to shed the excess.

A stenciled vine creates a framed background for this bed which is set on an angle.

Fabulous Fabrics

Many wallcovering collections come with coordinated fabrics that can be used for windows and bedspreads. However, you may choose to use special fabrics (especially sheet patterns) that capture your fancy. These, including juvenile designs, can be used as wallcovering as well. One advantage of using fabric is that you can build in soft padding that acts as a sound buffer insulation for children's walls.

Shirred Walls. Two notable techniques include shirring fabric onto curtain rods at the bottom and top of the wall (or above a wainscot), and using a padded wall system. For shirring, you will need at least two times the fabric (preferably three) of the width of the area to be covered. Allow enough fabric at the top and bottom to create a turned-over sleeve and hem for inserting the curtain rods. Shirred fabric walls are inappropriate for children's rooms where roughhousing is likely to take place. In addition, you may want to consider fireproofing the fabric before installing it. With these reservations in mind, shirred walls are extremely romantic for young girl's walls, and can be used to partially cover a wall for special effects. For instance, a shirred wall treatment behind a four-poster bed can be as romantic as a canopy bed treatment, and take up less precious floor space.

Padded fabric walls can be most easily applied through an ingenious track system. Batting is stapled to the wall, and a fabric-holding system is positioned on the wall where the edges of the fabric meet. Fabric is attached to the system and snapped into place.

Wallcovering: Ready-Made Patterns

If decorative painting isn't your forte, investigate wallcoverings. There are many collections specifically designed for children's rooms and nurseries, often pre-trimmed, prepasted and easy to use.

Most wallcoverings designed for children's rooms are scrubbable or washable. Often, various patterns are designed to coordinate so that you can combine a large-scale print with stripes or small-scale designs like geometrics. You can follow the suggested schemes of the wall-covering companies or mix and match your own combinations.

Wallcovering borders are specifically designed for use with wallcoverings, but also can be used to dress up painted walls. Use them to block off areas of the wall and create interest at a child's eye level.

One trick is to use general designs for the basic wallcovering, with strong themes in the borders. Border schemes include sports teams, rainbows, balloons, and popular cartoon characters. These can be replaced as a child grows, leaving the background wallcoverings intact.

Special pointers for using wallcoverings include the following:

■ Set off special areas by using a different wallcovering pattern. Many patterns come in a reverse version (dark color on light and light color on dark), ideally suited for setting off different areas cohesively.

■ Select themes that will be easily coordinated with the room's other elements, such as curtains and bedcovers.

■ If you anticipate scribbling, choose a wallcovering with a smooth surface that can easily be cleaned rather than a textured one that may be damaged by scrubbing.

■ Prepare the wall carefully. Sand and prime before applying wallcovering over all new surfaces.

Shirred and gathered fabric is used to set off the bed in this charming girl's room.

This Colorform border allows kids to move and restick add-on elements, providing hours of play. The city limits border is combined with a stripe.

Favorite teddy bears grace the border and wallcovering in a classic children's pattern.

Play Ball! An infield perspective for this larger-than-life photomural is many a Little Leaguer's dream.

Wallcovering Made Easy

Wallcovering is sold in rolls of various widths. Because patterns must be matched side to side along the edge of the strips, there is a fair amount of waste to keep the pattern repeating properly. To estimate material needs, as a general rule, determine the number of square feet in the area to be covered, less openings like windows and doors. Then divide this by 30, the usable square feet in a standard roll. Round up to the nearest whole number for ordering standard rolls. Consult your dealer to double-check how many you need. A repeating pattern also requires careful planning of where the job should start and end.

Where to Start

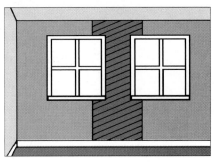

Start Over Door

Start in Dark Corner

When covering an entire room, it is unlikely that the pattern will line up perfectly. Plan so that separate strips meet at inconspicuous places, such as over a door or in a dark corner.

Use a roll of wallcovering as a measuring stick to divide the wall into increments as wide as the paper. If strips at either corner are less than half a roll wide, begin in the middle of the room.

Cut to Fit

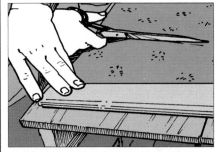

Measure for the Fit. Because wallcovering comes in rolls, it always must be cut to fit the height and width of the wall. Allow about 2" of overlap at the top and bottom to be trimmed off after the covering is on the wall. This lets you adjust a sheet up and down a little to meet the pattern properly.

Mark for Long Cuts. Long cuts on wallcovering should be marked at both ends, measuring in from the edge that will meet the piece already on the wall. Long cuts are usually made to fit the wallcovering into corners and should be measured from the top and bottom of the wall.

Paste Wallcovering

Mix the Paste. Wallcovering paste is available both premixed in liquid form and dry for mixing with water at home. If you are mixing your own, follow the manufacturer's instructions exactly. Work the powder into the water until it has a smooth, somewhat viscous consistency.

Apply the Paste. Lay a piece of the covering, cut to length, on a pasting table with one edge flush with a length of table edge. Paste the covering from table edge to the middle and about half its length. Then, repeat for the other side. This method prevents paste from getting on the tabletop.

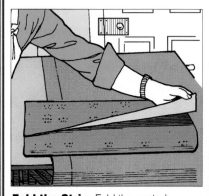

Fold the Strip. Fold the pasted section of a strip over on itself crosswise (paste to paste). Pull the remainder up on the table and paste the remaining section. Then, fold it into a manageable package and carry it to the wall. These packets can be set aside a few minutes to allow the paste to soften the covering.

Hang Wallcovering on the Wall

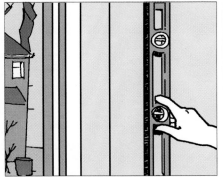

Find the Position. Decide at what point in the room you will start hanging the wallcovering and mark a vertical line at that point on the wall (in this case the starting point is along a window that is plumb). This guideline will establish the position of subsequent sheets.

Carry the Sheet to the Wall. Hold the sheet with top corners between thumb and forefinger, the rest of your hand supports the rest of the sheet. This enables you to position the paper at the top, allowing the rest of the sheet to fall into place.

Position the Covering. Put the top of the paper against the ceiling, leaving a few inches of overlap, and shift it into position along the vertical guideline (in the drawing, the edge of a window that is plumb). Let the rest of the strip drop down the wall.

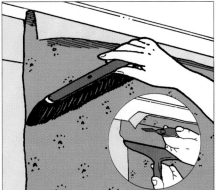

Brush and Trim. Once the strip is in position, use a wallcovering brush to smooth out wrinkles from the middle toward the edges and corners, smoothing top edge onto ceiling. Using a broadknife as a guide, trim with a razor knife. Wipe the surface with a sponge.

Hang Tight Seams

Butt the Edges. Position a second strip along the edge of the first so that the pattern lines up and the edges of the strips are butted together tightly with a very slight ridge at the junction. This ridge will subside.

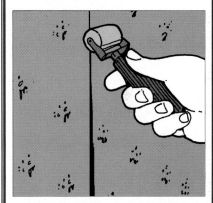

Press the Seam. When the paste has started to dry and the edges have sunk back, use a seam roller to flatten the seam and press the edges of the strips firmly into the paste. Roll once up and down. Do not repeat for you may create a shiny track.

Turn Inside Corners

Hang First Strip. Measure from the strip before a corner, to the corner at the top and bottom of the wall. Add 1/2" to the larger distance and transfer measurements to a strip. Cut lengthwise. Hang the new strip, letting the edge turn the corner. Brush it out. Tuck into the corner.

Mark Second Strip. Measure the width of the remaining section of covering and subtract 1/2". Transfer this measurement to the corner of the uncovered wall and use a plumb bob to find the vertical line. Mark this vertical as a guide for hanging the next piece.

Hang Second Strip. Hang the strip, positioning it against the line and brushing out as usual. Use the brush to tuck in the edge that meets the corner. Make diagonal cuts at the ceiling and baseboard to avoid wrinkling.

Playful Paneling

Subtle woodgrains and even some designs that look like wallcovering make paneling a wide open choice for children's rooms. Paneling, in 4' x 8' sheets, is a quick and easy way to cover a wall. Most paneling is prefinished and extremely durable in resisting scuffs and stains. Lightweight paneling often needs to be installed simply with adhesive rather than nails. Molding can cover top and bottom edges and ease the need for an extremely precise fitting.

Wood looks in both sheet paneling and paneling installed board by board offer decorative advantages. Wood is such a forgiving material that paneled walls can be used as giant bulletin boards. . . tack and nail holes will naturally be disguised within the woodgrain. The wood itself, either light toned or dark, serves as a neutral (though mostly masculine) background for the other decorative elements in the room.

Consider a wood look for children who have a love of nature and the environment. Wood is also good to give rooms a Southwestern aura and to decorate the play areas where you will be displaying various artworks and hanging objects. Other applications include whole walls of beaded board or

Both the borders and the green blackboard are situated at a child's eye level in this playroom.

wainscoting of this favorite turn of the century paneling, either in individual boards or in full-sized sheets. From clean Scandinavian and country looks to rugged bunkhouse wall treatments, be sure the wood paneling is splinter-free, then sit back and enjoy the childproof properties of paneling.

Activity Alternatives

You can encourage creativity by adding a pinup and blackboard section to the wall. School supply stores are good sources for blackboard-type materials, or the newer presentation boards that take special pens. The latter are best reserved for older children.

A less-costly alternative is to use blackboard paint available from paint stores. This paint can be applied directly to the wall. Use molding to set off areas reserved for activity. Kids who have a section of the wall set aside for their own use, to be redecorated whenever they wish with whatever they wish, can have hours of creative enjoyment with less temptation to deface the remaining walls.

Install Sheet Paneling with Adhesive

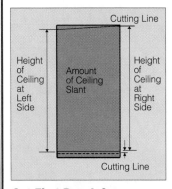

Cut First Panel. Start at a corner. Check wall for square at ceiling and floor. Measure height and cut panel 1/2" shorter for clearance. If wall is not square, measure the distance from the ceiling to floor where both edges of panel will sit; subtract 1/2".

Apply Adhesive. On a flat wall, cover surface with a random squiggle, and run a bead around the panel 1/2" from the edge. For unfinished or uneven walls nail furring strips to wall, then apply adhesive to furring.

Plumb Sheet. Set the panel against the wall, propped on wood shims and off the floor. Check the panel for plumb and correct the position. If panel is not plumb, remove and adjust it.

Conceal Seams. Use a felt-tip pen or paint, the same color as the grooves in the panels, to mark the surface along a seam before installing the next sheet. Install subsequent sheets.

Cork Bulletin Board

Every youngster needs a place to organize and pin up photographs, newspaper clippings, baseball cards, ribbons and so on, and this project fits the bill. The bulletin board is simply a frame made of scrap stock, molding, or picture-frame stock, holding a 1/4" hardboard back with cork tiles or sheet cork glued in place.

If the walls of your children's room are crowded, a good place to hang this bulletin board is on the inside of a closet door. True, it won't show off a collection as nicely as it would if it were hanging on the wall, but if the board is intended for reminders and other things that needn't be so public. Hanging it inside the closet uses an otherwise wasted space effectively. To mount the bulletin board, simply screw it onto a hardwood door or, in the case of a hollow-core door, use wall anchors short enough that they won't pierce the outside of the door.

An even simpler, equally effective closet-door bulletin board can be created by gluing cork tiles or sheet cork directly onto the door. In this way you can make a bulletin board as large as you wish in a matter of minutes. For gluing the cork to the door, follow the directions given in the last step of this project.

1. Cut the Frame. The materials listed here are for a 24" x 36" bulletin board, but the procedures are the same for any size. Use hardwood stock you have on hand, or buy picture-frame stock and cut it to the size you desire. Cut the pieces for the frame and use a table saw or radial arm saw to cut a 1/4" x 1/4" rabbet along the length of the inside back edges. Miter the corners at a 45-degree angle. Sand the pieces smooth.

2. Assemble the Board. Glue the corners of the frame together, making sure the frame is squared, and secure it in a picture-frame clamp. Allow to dry overnight. Cut the 1/4" hardboard to the dimensions given or, if you are making a larger or smaller bulletin board, to 1/2" longer and wider than the inside dimensions of the frame (so that it will fit into the rabbets). Glue the back into the frame and secure with small brass screws or brads for extra strength. Finally, finish the frame as you desire.

3. Apply the Cork. Use cork tiles, or sheet cork, if you can find it, for the face of the bulletin board. You will probably have to cut the tiles along two of the sides to fit inside the frame; the sheet cork can simply be cut to fit the whole area. To apply the cork, use contact adhesive or ordinary white glue. If you use white glue, press the tiles or sheet cork in place and hold them with weights, overnight, until dry.

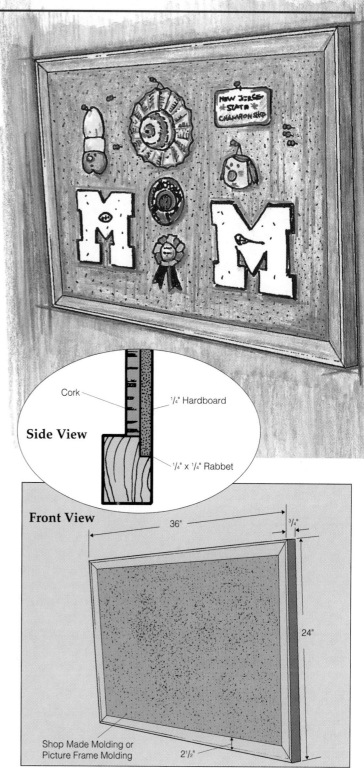

Cork

1/4" Hardboard

Side View

1/4" x 1/4" Rabbet

Front View

36"

3/4"

24"

2 1/2"

Shop Made Molding or Picture Frame Molding

Tools & Materials

- ☐ (2) 3/4" x 2 1/2" x 36" Any Hardwood Stock, Molding, or Picture-Frame Stock (For top and bottom of frame)
- ☐ (2) 3/4" x 2 1/2" x 24" Any Hardwood Stock, Molding, or Picture-Frame Stock (For frame ends)
- ☐ (1) 1/4" x 19 1/2" x 31 1/2" Hardboard (For back)
- ☐ Cork Tiles or Sheet Cork (Enough to make 19" x 31")
- ☐ Glue
- ☐ Contact Adhesive
- ☐ Brads or 1/2" Flathead Brass Screws
- ☐ Paint or Other Finish

Wonderful Window Treatments

The windows in children's rooms often are the major architectural features of the room. In many cases, there is only one window in a room of small proportion, so it takes on even greater significance. For these reasons, window treatments are extremely important in the overall scheme of a room. Windows also are among the first adventuring experiences of a child, since she can observe the greater world from the snug safety of her room.

The logical place to start assessing window needs is to consider physical properties. Then, make sure that the windows and their treatments are safe for kids. Knowing how to measure for various window treatments is essential before you set out for solutions. Then you can have fun selecting the blinds, shades, shutters, curtains or valences you want to use, either singly or layered.

Physical Properties

Consider your windows all day through, all year around. Window treatments can modify nature's effects to create an even and pleasant ambience within the room. You'll want to provide for adequate ventilation (when you want it), unimpeded by the window treatment. Conversely, you may need window treatments that will help cut down on winter drafts. For preschoolers, the ability to darken a room for naps is another important consideration. Your window treatment can even muffle some outside noises for naps or nighttime.

Having more than one window, particularly when they are on different walls, calls for compromising strategies. Often, matching combination window treatments (such as blinds plus curtains) work best in this situation. Each window treatment then can be operated according to the specific needs of the window. For instance,

A window seat covered with pillows and a double window treatment of fabric valance and Roman shades create a unified area. The Roman shades will darken the room completely.

sun-blocking curtains can be drawn over a western window during nap time, while the curtains are left open on the room's northern wall and blinds are lowered but remain open for ventilation. There are attractive solutions to suit every need and style.

If there's a chance that you might replace the windows themselves for more energy efficient models, plan your window treatments to suit the new replacements. For instance, an inside mounted blind on the old window may not work as well if reinstalled in a new, thicker window.

Window Safety

Window guard rails are not only a good idea, then are legally necessary in some localities. Call your local housing bureau to see which standards they recommend or mandate. One recommended design factor is that the rail not have horizontal bars that a child could climb upon to get up above the rail. This is a self-defeating design.

The safest windows themselves are those that have a plastic core similar to those used in windshields of cars, so that the windows will not shatter if broken. Less expensive than a full

replacement, you can install a rigid plastic liner inside a conventional window if you fear that your child might break the glass.

Anderson windows, in conjunction with the Screen Manufacturers Association, has launched an awareness campaign to let everyone know that most window screens are NOT designed to keep children from falling out of windows. Parents must take other safety measures to protect their children. The following are a few helpful tips.

■ Whenever small children are around, close and lock windows. If you need ventilation, open windows that children cannot reach, for example, open double-hung windows from the top only (unless you have a guard rail in place).

■ Keep furniture away from windows. Children can climb to window ledges or sills and then fall.

■ Keep window treatments out of children's reach, so they cannot use them to climb or accidentally choke themselves (blinds, cords and drapes all are potential hazards).

■ Leave cranks on casement and awning windows unless you know they will not be needed for an emergency exit. Cap the exposed studs with covers from the manufacturer if you do remove the cranks (so children can't open them themselves).

■ Make sure children know which windows (or other exits) are best for use in case of fire, and make sure children old enough have practiced exiting according to your plan.

■ Be sure you can open windows in an emergency. Do not paint, nail or weatherstrip windows shut, or cover them with a window treatment (such as shutters) that makes an emergency exit impossible.

■ Keep kids away from windows and patio doors when they roughhouse.

Treatments Made to Measure

While a number of window treatments can be custom made to fit your child's room, ready-made options are handy and available as well. Sources include local furnishing and linen stores as well as a number of catalogue merchants. Often, a favorite bedspread or crib cover comes with coordinated window curtains. And if they don't, you can craft your own curtains from such easy resources as pillowcases, sheets, fabric or towels.

Key to any successful window treatment is accurate measurement and planning of the size of the treatment. You should be familiar with the standard measurements that follow.

Width. Curtains, blinds and shutters can be placed inside a window frame, at the outer edge of the window frame, or "cheated" on the wall (covering the frame) to make the window appear wider than it is. Confine the window treatment to the frame if you don't want to block the view, or if you want to get the most possible natural light. Bring an overly large-scaled window into line by minimizing its window treatment with placement inside the frame.

Length. Window treatments can be placed inside the frame's top edge to sill height. Or, treatments can start at the top of the frame and extend to the apron of the frame or to the floor. These are conventional lengths that visually anchor the treatment to the window.

Window treatments can start above the window frame, so long as they cover the frame. The effect then is of a window with a shade or curtain partially lowered. A winning combination for almost any child's room is to use blinds with a curtain treatment that is confined to the

upper part of the window. Swags, balloon shades, roman shades and valences all fit this category. The curtains provide the decorative accent that is safely out of the way of mischievous hands.

Exterior Considerations. Inside frame window treatments usually allow for a leakage of light around the perimeter. Window coverings that go to the outside of the frame provide a tighter seal for both light and air.

Give thought also to the look of your window treatment from the outside. If the curtains are decorated with a strong children's pattern that may be jarring from the outside, you will probably want to line them with a more suitably colored fabric. A case in point would be a strong, primary-colored balloon pattern in a child's room positioned directly over the front door.

Successful Window Treatments

Blinds, shades, shutters and curtains, used alone or topped with valences or cornices, make up a window's wardrobe. Layered looks are both practical and pretty. Most often, you will find blinds combined with curtains.

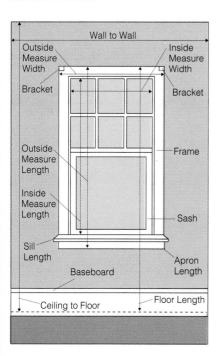

Out of reach but affording some decoration, the balloon shade fabric coordinates with the rest of the patterns used throughout the room.

Blinds offer the versatility and ventilation that is perfect for many children's rooms. Here, traditional blinds are topped with a romantic fabric treatment to set off a window seat.

the blind itself. Or, you might take elements from a curtain treatment and decoupage them onto the blinds for a unique look.

Designs for specific applications include metallic reflector blinds that help keep sun's rays bounced back to the outside at the same time that they admit breezes. Conversely, deep-toned blinds that absorb heat can be set to gather in the warmth of the sun. Some perforated blinds are designed to provide privacy but allow for air circulation even if fully closed.

Pleated shades provide a softer look to windows. Hybrid shade-and-blind combinations can give the advantages of a softer

window look with the ability to totally darken a room. Pleated shades are available in a range of insulation and draft-proof levels, from those that add very little to those that trap air spaces to increase the insulating "R" value of the window itself.

Some window manufacturers incorporate shades into the structure of the window. Protecting the blinds behind glass eliminates the need for dusting, which can be a chore with miniblinds. Integrated blinds are clear advantages for slanted windows or skylights, since they will hang on an angle that matches the window. Many blinds (even inexpensive ones) come with optional hardware to use in attaching them to the bottom of the window, an easy solution for slanted windows.

Blinds and Shades. An ideal choice where ventilation and versatility are issues, window blinds date back to the beginning of the United States. The older style 2" taped wood blinds are returning to popularity in painted, stained and sealed wood variations. Because of their place in history, these blinds are good choices for traditionally styled or country styled homes. But don't overlook the many modern blind styles that offer special advantages you may want.

Narrow blinds visually are less imposing than broad blinds. They also give a more modern look to any room. Manufacturers have special custom programs that enable you to not only color match exactly, but to vary colors within the blinds. For instance, blinds can be made to your specifications with stripes of different colors as well as solids. Some manufacturers also offer textures such as woodgrains on mini-blinds, or linen looks.

You can paint or add decals to blinds yourself to personalize your shades. For example, you might extend a stenciled treatment of leaves and vines that surrounds a window onto

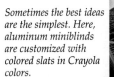

Sometimes the best ideas are the simplest. Here, aluminum miniblinds are customized with colored slats in Crayola colors.

Like blinds, shades can be customized and even come in ready-made patterns, such as this one.

It's also possible to have shades and blinds that draw up from the bottom, instead of being suspended from the top. Consider these when you want privacy but would like to maintain a view of the sky above. Be sure that the raising and lowering mechanisms are childproof.

If ventilation is not a consideration for you but darkness for nap time is, consider old-fashioned window shades. Available in many department and general stores, opaque shades are the most dense window treatments. Translucent shades that provide light but block the view may be a good solution for children who need to rest but do not like total darkness.

In selecting either blinds or shades, the more benefits built into the product, the higher the price. More expensive options include custom sizes, custom colors and designs, heavier weight of blinds, specialty fabrics for shades, and custom shapes to fit unusually shaped windows. The least expensive choices include plain shades or those blinds offered in stock widths and colors (white, beige, sometimes grey). Such unobtrusive colors are not only most economical, they transmit the sunlight into the room with the least amount of color distortion (in comparison to shades of more distinctive hues).

Shutters are another option that works beautifully in kid's rooms. Fixed louvers will take more abuse than the adjustable styles. They also provide ventilation while dressing the window. Other options, for a softer look, include shutters with shirred fabric inserts. Either is a good option for traditionally styled rooms, and can visually take up little space when set into a deep-set window.

Curtains to Charm Kids. While shutters, shades and blinds add a linear crispness to windows, curtains add a softened charm. A first consideration is to balance the visual impact of the window and its curtains with the rest of the room. For instance, if you have a girl's room with a canopied bed, multiple

A valance and bedspread in matching fabrics are teamed with a shade in the fabric's background color.

When a room is cut up with many angles and nooks, capitalizing on a window feature with a strong curtain treatment can give it the design focus it needs, as was done here with a double dormer.

pillows and dust ruffles, the fabric at the windows should be of equal fullness and weight. Conversely, a window treatment that is very full in a strictly contemporary, Spartan room will seem out of step and out of scale. One good rule of thumb, especially in children's rooms, is to use less fabric but in a generous way. For instance, rather

The fanciful walls found in this elegant nursery call for restrained treatment on the French doors. Note the simple swags on the porch windows; an echo of tasteful restraint.

than opting for skinny curtains on either side of the window, you may want to use an ample balloon shade. The same amount of fabric used this way packs more visual punch. Choices for curtains include a wealth of ready-made styles as well as those you can simply make yourself. Of the former, use the directions on the back of the packages that tell you what size to use to fit your window. But don't be limited to that assessment; you may find that you want to use a wider width to create a pleasing fullness.

If you are at all handy with a sewing machine, you'll find that you can make curtains with little effort. You even can find patterns for swags, ruffled curtains and cafe curtains. Here are some pointers and suggestions for both ready-made curtains and those you make from scratch.

■ Sheets and pillowcases can be made into curtains. The borders can be used as tiebacks, and the rolled over hems can be used as the sleeve for the curtain rod. To hem bottoms, use self-stick sewing tape (if you don't want to bother sewing them).

■ Roman shades (that pull up with overlapping flat panels) and balloon shades (that pull up in gathered sections along shirred strips) can be created with ready-made tapes that have the gathering or folding intervals built in. In fact, some of these tapes are self-sticking when you iron them on.

■ Both Roman and balloon shades look fine used alone at the top of a window, or combined with a blind. Installations such as this are ideal for toddler's rooms, to give windows softness in a treatment out of a child's reach.

■ Consider other window-topping treatments. Among these is a simple swag, which can be arranged over hooks at either side of the window or entwined over a curtain rod. Make sure that the "tails" of the swag reach at least down to the top 1/3 of the window's frame so that they don't look skimpy.

■ Fabric valances at a window's top, especially those with a deep hem beneath the rod, add softness. For even more fullness, add tissue inside the doubled width.

■ When matching windows of different heights, mount the curtain at the same height on the wall to make them look compatible.

■ Create a crown, molding-like detail on a window treatment, by creating a wood valence and stenciling it to match draperies. Or, cover a simple board with fabric to match cafe curtains to top off the window and balance the treatment. Another alternative is to stencil or use wallcovering borders to decorate a valance to match the curtains.

■ Create your own special window effect by making a plywood frame to fit entirely around the window. Decorate this with paint to match or contrast with curtains or blinds.

High-hanging lighting fixtures are balanced by the slash of horizontal color that divides the walls and blind. Using overhead lights is a safe choice since there are no wires underfoot to worry about.

Lighting it Right

A child's bright, inquisitive eyes are ready to read, ready to play and ready to participate in all sorts of hobbies. In order to accomplish all of this activity, it is very important that the appropriate lighting is provided. Children react to the lighting in the room more than any other single factor. After all, as long as the room is not entirely dark, the child will trust that no monsters are present.

Lighting can make the color in a room come alive. On the other hand, improper lighting will create a mute, drab environment. An absorbing hobby that requires much detail work will be a pleasure with good lighting, a fatiguing chore with inadequate lighting. Physically and psychologically, planning the lighting in a child's room is extremely important, and all too frequently overlooked.

There are many things you will need to know as you develop a lighting scheme. Among them are the function of light, the types of effective lighting, how to meld artificial and natural light, those tasks that need specific lighting support, the benefits and uses of types of light fixtures, how to develop a lighting layout and room plan, and for the adventurous, suggestions on do-it-yourself lighting.

Lighting needs will change as your child grows. The first nursery stages require ample lighting above the changing area, general overall lighting, and a soft night-light that can be left on for the frequent nightly tending a child requires. By the middle school years, the same child's room will probably need task lighting for studying and reading, and could benefit from the use of accent lighting to show off a special collection or hobby. So, plan your lighting with the knowledge that it should be flexible to suit changing needs.

If you absolutely need light and there's no wiring, this nursery light operates on two "C" batteries, and can be mounted to changing tables, cribs or the wall.

Lighting Functions

Children's rooms call for a combination of the basic lighting types: general lighting, task lighting and accent lighting.

General Lighting. This type of lighting is the overall illumination that provides the background for the other forms of lighting. It can be accomplished by ceiling or wall-mounted fixtures, with recessed or track lights, and often is attached to a switch near the door so that you can switch on the light to safely traverse the room. . . whether toys have been put away or not. It's necessary to create a comfortable level of brightness without producing a glare or overlighting the area.

Task Lighting. Used to direct light to the specific areas needed to perform a task, task lighting is most often provided by portable lamps, track and recessed lights. In children's rooms, tasks include changing and dressing a baby, reading to a child, all kids' activities that are "close" (such as looking at picture books, drawing and homework), reading and crafts or hobbies. The lighting fixture itself should focus light where needed, without creating glare itself or in the reflection off a work surface. Shadowless illumination helps prevent eyestrain and discomfort. Kids who don't have well-lit study areas are at a distinct disadvantage to those who do.

Accent Lighting. The drama-maker in a child's room, accent lighting is designed to spotlight a specific object or to create a special effect. It should be at least three times as strong as the general lighting. Daylight accent lighting can highlight a trophy or pennant, collection or favorite poster or painting. A lower intensity can serve as an accent light when the rest of the room is dark, providing an accent and night-light in one. Track lighting, recessed lighting and wall-mounted fixtures, as well as freestanding or clip-on spotlights, can serve to create accent lighting.

Types of Light

The sources of light—the bulbs—are available in a many different forms, each having its own advantages. The way to compare bulbs is to consider their wattage, which is the electricity consumed by the bulb, versus the lumens, which is the amount of light the bulb gives off. Footcandles represent the amount of light reaching a subject, measured at the subject.

Small-scale, targeted spotlights can create more footcandles of light on a subject (such as a bulletin board) using less wattage and lumens than light from a bulb that isn't directed. For instance, a 50 watt "R" bulb can put as much footcandle light on an object as a 100 watt "A" bulb (definitions to follow). Highly efficient fluorescent lights can flood an area with light using lower wattage than incandescent lamps, when both produce the same lumens.

General Bulbs (A). Look for energy-saving general bulbs, also known as "A" bulbs, that provide longer life and less need for replacement. These are conventionally used in portable lamps. Globe styles (G) in lower wattages can be used without producing too much glare. Some specialty bulbs are silvered on top to cut down on glare when seen from the top of lamps.

Reflector Bulbs (R). The shape of these bulbs creates a reflector that directs light and concentrates it forward. Floodlight reflectors (FL) spread light, while spotlight reflectors (SP) concentrate the light. Using reflectors in a fixture puts approximately double the amount of light on a subject as an "A" bulb of the same wattage, because the light is more concentrated. Parabolic reflectors (PAR) are even more efficient, producing about four times the light of an "A" bulb.

Tungsten-Halogen (T) Bulbs. Often used for accent lights and for task lamps, they produce a "white" light close to the look of sunlight, and are about 10 percent brighter than incandescent lights of equal wattage. Although they are more expensive, they last about three to four times longer. Some halogen lights are designed to fit right into conventional light fixtures and have shatterproof bulbs. These are classified as "A" line halogens. Others may require special sockets. The sturdier bulbs that are shatterproof are most suitable for any area where children could come into contact with the lamps or bulbs.

Fluorescent Bulbs. Take a new look at fluorescent bulbs, because they are vastly improved from even a few years ago. First, the flickering that was so annoying has been eliminated in many models, and the harsh color can be avoided, by selecting deluxe warm white tones that emulate incandescent light. Fluorescents remain the best energy savers, since they draw as much as 1/3 to 1/6th of the wattage of incandescent lights for the same lumens. Fluorescents can be used for

Install Fluorescent Fixtures

The three parts of a fluorescent fixture are the tube, which may be straight or circular, the starter and the ballast.

Inside the tube, an electric current arcs from a cathode at one end of the tube to an anode at the other. The tube is filled with mercury and argon gases. As the arc passes through the gases, it causes them to emit invisible ultraviolet light. The inside of the tube is coated with phosphor powder that glows when hit by ultraviolet light.

The starter is a switch that closes when activated by an electric current. After a momentary delay, the starter allows current to energize gases in the tube.

The ballast is a box-like component usually about 6" to 7" long. It monitors electrical current so that it is at the level required to provide proper light operation. When the light is turned on, a transformer steps up the voltage to deliver a momentarily high surge of electricity, causing the tube to glow.

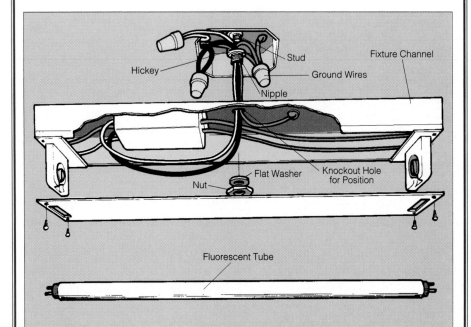

One-Tube Fixtures. If the box has a stud, you will need a hickey and nipple. If not, you can attach the fixture to a nipple and strap screw it to the ears in the box. First splice the fixture wires to the house wires, attach wire connectors, and wrap the splices with plastic electrical tape. Then attach the fixture to the box with the nipple, a washer and a locknut. Have a helper hold the fixture while you assemble and fasten it to the box. When the fixture is stable, drive a couple of sheet-metal screws through the fixture housing at each end. Knockouts in housing let you position fixture almost anywhere over the box. Punch out the knockout. Connect the wiring. Fasten to the wall or ceiling. Add screws through the housing at ends to support the fixture.

recessed lighting, to wash walls with light, and for task lighting. Usual configurations are those that require a specific fluorescent fixture in either a bar or circular pattern.

Compact Fluorescents. These bulbs are almost too good to be true. Often designed to fit into conventional screw-in "A" bulb fixtures, compact fluorescent lights more than make up for their hefty initial cost through the savings in energy and in the ecology that

they provide through their lifetimes. These units are composed of a ballast (regulating the electricity) and fluorescent tubes that have been bent, much as a french horn or trombone evolved. It's the bending of the tube that makes the bulbs fit conventional lamps, and the computerized ballast that makes them feasible, according to Osram, who specializes in compact fluorescents.

When using compact bulbs instead of incandescent bulbs, there are some things to consider. These bulbs are so efficient that they stay cool, so a child is unlikely to get burned if she touches them. They are heavier than conventional bulbs and must be used in fixtures where weight is no problem (such as an overhead fixture or wall sconce), or in a standing or portable lamp that is heavily weighted in the base. Try tipping a lamp yourself to see if it still resists toppling with the addition of the heavier bulb. Modifications have even adapted these bulbs to use as a three-way fixture or in dimmer stages. It is best to use these bulbs in places where lights will be left on for a long time (over three hours at a stretch), since this helps assure their long life.

Styles with diffusing globes covering the tubes provide the softest light, and may be the best choice if you do see the bulb itself. Logical applications include night-lights or lights used for ambient lighting throughout the day or evening.

Two-Part Compact Fluorescents. While most compact fluorescents have the ballast and tubes permanently attached, these units are separated. The ballasts outlast the tubes by about three or four to one, and accept replacement tubes. Over time this is less costly, and also creates less waste in the landfill for the ecologically minded.

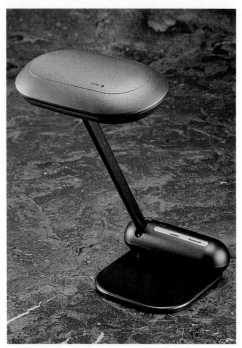

This desk lamp is designed to utilize compact fluorescent bulbs. For optimum weight balance, the ballast has been built into the lamp base, creating a contemporary look.

Fluorescent Savings

If you are an environmentally concerned parent (as are most these days), here are some figures from Sylvania concerning compact fluorescent lights. By using one 18-watt compact fluorescent instead of a 75-watt incandescent, you will affect the following savings:

■ One compact fluorescent bulb lasts an average of 10,000 hours, which means it replaces approximately 13 incandescent bulbs in its lifetime. Since bulbs cannot be recycled, this saves on the addition to dumps.

■ Less electricity is being used during this bulb's 10,000 hours, so there's a corresponding reduction of average emissions of Carbon Dioxide (greenhouse effect), 912 lbs., Nitrogen Oxide (smog), 3.5 lbs, and Sulfur Dioxide (acid rain), 6.6 lbs.

■ Since less electricity is used, less fossil fuel is needed to produce that electricity; in fact, there's a savings of (depending upon which is used to create the electricity), 530 lbs of coal,

40 gallons of oil or 6100 cubic feet of natural gas.

■ While the initial cost of the bulbs is considerably higher than conventional incandescents (about $15 to $25 per bulb on average), you'll save an average of at least $25 per bulb.

Broken down, this savings results from not having to purchase the 13 other bulbs (about $13 on average), plus the savings on your electric bill. The chart below shows how using more efficient bulbs can affect the cost of lighting your child's room.

Light Bulb Energy Savings Chart

Incandescent Wattage	Replace with Fluorescent	Savings on Electricity[1]
2-60W	2-20W Tubes	$84.00
1-100W	2-20W Tubes	$60.00
2-75W	4-20W Tubes	$60.00
1-60W	1-32W Circline	$28.00
3-60W	1-32/40W Circline	$120.00
1-75W	1-18W "U" Bulb	$31.20[2]
1-75W	2-PL-7W Compact	$51.00[3]
2-75W	2-PL-13W Compact	$114.00[3]

(1) Includes allowance for ballast wattage. Calculated @ 10¢ per KWH for rated lamp life of 12,000 hours.
(2) Calculated on 8,000 hour rated lamp life.
(3) Calculated on 10,000 hour rated lamp life.

Types of Fixtures

The effectiveness of lighting is a function of both bulbs and fixtures. There are some general rules concerning which fixtures to use and how to use them effectively.

Track Lighting. To wash a wall with light, you will want to space the track 2' to 3' from the wall on ceilings up to 9' high. Mount tracks 3' to 4' on ceilings 9' to 11' high. Space the fixtures the same distance apart as the track is from the wall. To accent specific objects with track lights, fixtures should be aimed at a 30-degree angle from the vertical to prevent light from shining in eyes, and to avoid glare caused by reflections. To determine the best placement see the drawing below and follow these steps:

1. Measure the distance (B to C) from the ceiling to the center of the object to be accented.

2. Mount the track at location A, which is the distance (A to B), from the wall along the ceiling, see table. For instance, if the distance to the center of a bulletin board is 4', then the accent light should be mounted 27" from the wall on the ceiling.

A to B Location In Inches	B to C Distance In Feet
13"	2 ft.
20"	3 ft.
27"	4 ft.
34"	5 ft.
41"	6 ft.

Install Track Lights

Be sure to turn off the circuit on which you will be working. Roughly plot the position of the track on the ceiling. Install a ceiling junction box, if none exists, at one end of the track's location and fish cable to the box. If you are using a plug-in track lighting system, install the track, then simply plug it into an existing outlet.

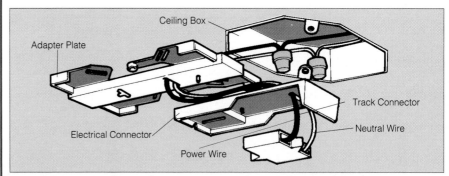

Install Connector Plate. Connect the track wiring to the house wiring using the metal adaptor plate. Use wire connectors to connect like-colored wires; hook up the track wires to the cable wires. Fasten adapter assembly to junction box ears with screws.

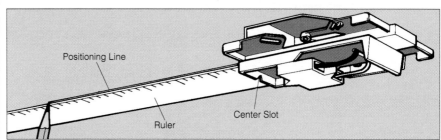

Plot the Track. To plot the line for the track itself, align a ruler with the center slot on the track connector. Draw the line straight across the ceiling to the location of the opposite end of the track.

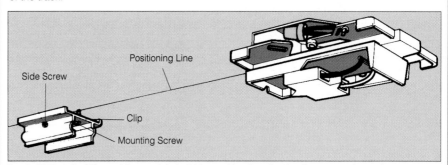

Install Track Clips. The track is held in position by plastic clips spaced evenly across the line. Center the clip on the line and draw a mark for the screw hole. Install clips using toggle bolts (for drywall) or wood screws (for wood).

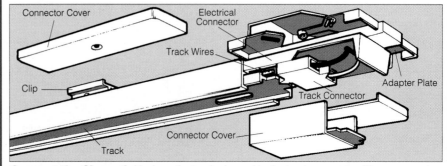

Connect the Channel. Hook up the track channel to the track connector. Then, connect the track connector to the electrical connector. Snap the track channels into the clips. Tighten the setscrews to hold channels in position. Install raceway cover, and attach the track lights.

Recessed Lighting. Cone, baffle, diffused or concentrated lens fixtures all can amplify or diminish the effectiveness of either general "A" bulbs or targeted "R" or "PAR" lights. Generally, you will want to have 15-25 footcandles of light generated by recessed lighting.

Manufacturers, designers and lighting retailers can tell you how many square feet will be covered by a specific fixture and bulb type. This enables you to plan the recessed lighting layout before installing them. For instance, a diffused recessed light with a 75-watt "A" bulb covers 20 square feet. Therefore, you might plan on dividing a child's room that's 8' x 10' by sectioning it into equal quarters measuring 4' x 5' (20 square feet), and centering the recessed lights within these quarters. In this case, lights would be placed 2' in from the 8' sides of the room, and 2$\frac{1}{2}$' in from the longer 10' walls.

To use recessed lighting to wash walls, space lights the same distance apart as the distance they are from the wall to be washed. For medium level light (15-20 footcandles) use 100-watt "A" bulbs evenly spaced 2' apart or 150-watt "A" bulbs spaced 4' apart, or 150-watt "R" bulbs at 3' intervals. For high levels (30-45 footcandles) space either 120-watt bulb 2' apart.

Wall Lighting. Charming wall lamps dressed up with childhood motifs range from balloon designs to contemporary themes and are wonderful decorative accents. They also perform as an effective source of lighting. Since rooms seem larger when walls are well lit, decorative wall lamps should be used to direct diffused light to the walls.

Other wall lighting fixtures combine general lighting functions with specific task lighting. A wall-mounted lamp is a good choice in smaller areas, where you want to eliminate desktop clutter, or to accommodate the top bunk occupant. For task use, the best choice is an adjustable three-way lamp that swings out on an arm. You may want a top shield and a bottom diffuser if the shade is shallow.

Fluorescent wall fixtures also provide out-of-the-way light sources that can be effectively positioned above worktables or desks. Light can be directed downward or up and down.

Wall lamps should have switches that are easy for a child to reach as soon as she is old enough to turn on the lights.

With any electrical cords, especially lamp cords, care must be taken to put them in a safe out-of-the way place. Any wall lamp can be outfitted with a safety track that covers the cord and attaches to the wall.

Portable Lamps. Available in classic or children's styles, these lamps light approximately 40 to 50 square feet of area, and usually only service one individual's activities as a task light. However, four or five portable lamps strategically placed will meld into overall ambient lighting.

Consider adult lighting needs in the room. You will want a reading light near a chair in a nursery or young child's room as well as good lighting over the changing table. You may want a night-light, or a very low setting on a three-way lamp. And for cleaning, you will need overall lighting of relatively high intensity.

Portable lights for adult reading should be positioned so that the bottom of the shade is just at eye height when seated (about 38" to 42" above the floor). The shorter the table, the taller the lamp should be.

Keep in mind that adult eyes need 25 percent more light for tasks than young eyes, and that what may be comfortable for you might be overly bright for a child. In the same vein, make sure that opaque diffusers or globes are used in the lamp you select for adult use. It will prevent children, who will be situated at a lower level, from peering straight into the bulb.

Shades. In general, a lamp should have a shade with at least a 16" opening at the bottom for sufficient lighting. The bulb in an upright socket should line up with the bottom of the shade. Deep shades may require longer harps or a recessed top

fitting to position the socket correctly.

General Electric recommends open-top, white or light-neutral colored translucent shades to maximize light utilization while assuring visual comfort. Vinyl, parchment, fabric laminates or fairly dense white-lined fabric shades are recommended. Colored shades that tint the light can create havoc with your color scheme, since they distort the room's colors. Rooms look best when all shades are at roughly the same height.

Dense or opaque shades are recommended only in rooms in which the walls are dark. However, if you have two children sharing a room, providing nighttime reading lights with opaque shades may be the best way of making sure that the light from one reading child won't disturb the other child. During regular activity, these directional lights should always be used in conjunction with other lamps.

For safety sake, remove plastic wrappers from lamp shades. Do not use light bulbs of a higher wattage than shown on the socket or tag when purchasing the lamp. Mark the wattage on the socket if you remove the tag, for future reference.

Efficiency. Three-way lamps and dimmers enable you to use only the amount of electricity you want so you can turn the lamp to lower wattage settings when a task is over.

Placing lamps where they will bounce light off walls, magnifying it, is more energy efficient. Finally, outfit ambient portable lamps which will rarely be used for task lighting with energy-saving bulbs of lower wattage than conventional bulbs.

Lighting for Tasks. Which chores and hobbies are most demanding of light? Sewing tops most lists, since it involves matching a thread color to a background (black on black, white on white). If your child develops an interest in a hobby as visually demanding as this, make sure that you increase the task lighting to fit this new demand.

Lighting Needs

The different types of lighting can be combined so that all lighting needs are covered. Here are some general guidelines of ways to meet the tasks kids undertake.

Table Lamps for Reading. The shade top can be 8" to 17", height 10" to 20" and bottom opening 16" to 18". Use bulbs for casual use, 150 watts, extending to 170, 200 and 250 for prolonged use. Locate the base in line with the shoulder, 20" to the right or left center of a book.

Generally, wall, swag or floor lamps are set with the shade bottom at 40" to 47" high. Floor lamps are probably not as safe in a child's room as other styles unless well away from play and traffic patterns.

Lamps for Reading in Bed. Decide whether you want to have the lamp to read to the child snuggled next to him, or whether the lamp is for the child himself. This determines the best height. For semi-reclining, the bottom of the shade should be at eye level. Put the lamp in line with the shoulder about 22" to the side of the center of the book.

Usually 20" to 24" is a good height for adults. To determine the best height for your child, have him get comfortable in the bed, then take note of his eye level. The lamp must be an easy reach from the bed.

Desk Work. A variety of lighting types work well for desks. A desk lamp should have a low brightness shade with a white or near-white interior. The bottom of the shade should be 15" above the work surface. Position the lamp 15" to one side of center of the work and 12" back from the front edge of the desk. Locate it to the left for right-handed kids, and right for a left-handed one. Use lamps that go up to 250 watts for intense paperwork, though 100 watts is usually most comfortable.

A pair of wall lamps provides good overlap light and covers large areas eliminating veiling glare. Locate the bottom of the shades 15" above the work surface, centered 30" apart and

use 100 watt bulbs in each for casual work, up to 150 watts for detail work, for desks 20" to 22" deep. For a standard-size desk, center lamps 36" apart and not more than 17" from the front edge of the desk.

Visual Display Terminals. Adjustable lamps are best because lighting needs to light up the keyboard and written material, but not the child or monitor screen. Adjustable lamps allow the child to position the lamp wherever it will do the job best, which may change with the type of equipment he uses and his positioning as he grows. Sylvania suggests that the light sources are best placed above or beside the terminal, which washes light over the wall, diffusing it for the work space.

Glare from other lights or windows can further add to visual display fatigue. To check for glare, move a small pocket mirror across the computer screen. If you see a bright reflection, adjust the lamps or screen until the reflection disappears.

Hobbies and Crafts. For detailed work such as model building, needlework, fabric painting, stamp or coin collecting, a combination of good task lighting and supplementary lighting may be necessary. Task lighting positioned similarly to desk lighting forms the basis. A supplementary table lamp or a directional lamp aimed at the work adds illumination and allows shadows that can help differentiate details. Place this lamp to the side of the work area, towards the front of the table, and direct it towards the work.

Natural Effects. In addition to lamps, natural lighting works its own magic in a child's room. Take the natural lighting into account when planning the lighting scheme and furniture arrangements, especially if a child uses the room predominantly in the daytime.

On the positive side, natural lighting is free illumination. You can use it by arranging furniture so that the play area, especially the floor of a toddler's room or a play table, are

naturally lit. Conversely, be sure that natural light sources do not create glare on work or study areas. For instance, do not place a desk facing into a window, where glare will inevitably flow onto the work surface in daylight hours. Placing it at right angles means the light can be used without the glare. A desk that is lit naturally from behind, will cast a shadow onto the child's work. However, an artificial light can be used to properly balance out the natural light.

Use other natural phenomena to your advantage by considering the reflection of light off of various surfaces. For instance, be sure that the wall behind a desk (especially with a computer monitor) is light colored. The desk surface itself should be light colored as well. Solve the problem of a dark colored desk by providing a light blotter. If you have selected a dark color scheme, increase the lumens to maintain a comfortable light level. This combats the natural tendency of dark colors to absorb and muffle light, while light colors reflect it and therefore magnify it.

Create a Lighting Plan

Armed with a good idea of the needs of your children's room, you are ready to make a plan. First map out the furniture, then add the lighting you have, marking all the outlets. Use the 1/4" grid that you use for furniture layouts and the furniture templates found in Appendix A. Make cutouts to represent the various kinds of lighting you are considering. You can place them with the furniture and then adjust the plan until it's perfect.

Safety considerations that should be built into the plan include a lamp that can be lit from the doorway, so no one has to enter the room in the dark. And unless a night-light is used, an easy-to-reach, bedside lamp is a must.

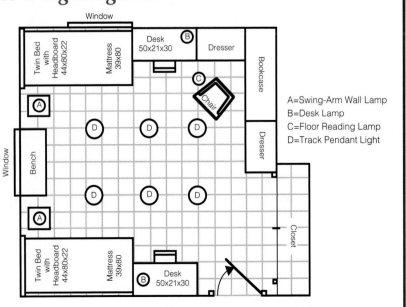

A=Swing-Arm Wall Lamp
B=Desk Lamp
C=Floor Reading Lamp
D=Track Pendant Light

Comfort Controls

Heating and ventilation are important in any child's room, and especially in a nursery. Checking for drafts and knowing how to regulate air circulation are the first steps to controlling the atmosphere. Once you've determined these factors, you can develop a plan to provide heat or air conditioning that will keep a kid's room most comfortable.

Beating the Draft

Windows are obvious sources of drafts, but so are baseboards in many older homes. Since cold air drops down, and children practically live on the floor during the early years, check for drafts at floor level as well as around windows.

One way to check drafts is to use a candle to determine the source of a draft—it will blow the flame in the opposite direction. Check your electrical outlets as part of your audit, since they are often a source of heat loss. If the outlets are a source of drafts, you can install insulating pads to create a barrier (turn off the power before attempting this and other jobs that concern electricity).

Baseboards. Drafts coming from beneath the baseboard can result from insulation that does not fit

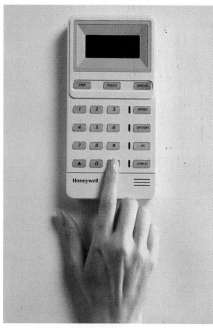

Look for systems that control heat, cooling, warnings of fire and smoke, appliances, and lighting, all in one such as this console.

properly with sufficient snugness at the bottom. Run weather stripping below the baseboard, or for a really good job, remove the baseboard and add insulation as needed. Prior to adding the insulation, make sure that there is not an opening from the outside that should be caulked.

Another method of eliminating floor drafts is to create carpeted baseboards. This treatment, borrowed from Europe, is especially handsome in kid's rooms where the entire floor is carpeted and acts as a play space. The carpeting is installed, then strips 3" to 6" wide are finished on the top edge. These are butted to the carpeting on the floor, creating a right angle that surrounds the entire room with a carpet baseboard. Tacks, carpet tape and carpet adhesive are all appropriate means of attaching the baseboard, depending upon the weight of the carpeting.

Windows. In addition to the replacement of faulty, drafty windows, there are some other techniques that can help with drafty windows. Make sure all cracks are sealed around the window, and apply weather stripping as needed by season and weather. A simple solution for windows you open is to make a strip of stuffed fabric in a roll, like the Colonial door draft keepers. Use these in the middle of the sash or at the bottom, wherever needed. In selecting window treatments, consider their sun-reflecting or draft-preventing properties, depending upon which you need most.

Make sure that window air conditioners are either removed in winter or that you cover them with draft-hindering materials.

Air Conditioners. Most machines come with adjustable louvers that enable you to deflect air. However, they may not be powerful enough to prevent a draft. Deflecting screens can be used to keep a blast from an air conditioner away from playing or sleeping children. The solution can be as simple as a folding screen directly in front of the air conditioner but about 1' from its face.

Window treatments offer a good way of increasing insulation and avoiding drafts, in products such as an insulated blind and valence combination.

Healthy Heat

Newborn's rooms should be maintained at about 80°F since babies cannot regulate body temperatures or cover themselves. From the toddler age forward, a child's room can be kept at the same temperature as the rest of the home.

If you need supplementary heating for a child's room, its most efficient placement is below a window which probably is the source of most drafts and heat loss. Both permanent and portable heating units throughout the house must be screened by a barrier that prevents a child from touching and being burned by them. This is especially important during the crawling years.

For old-fashioned radiators, using a cover allows the warmth to get out but keeps children from reaching anything hot. Baseboard heating systems should be upgraded with child-resistant covers, too. Consult heat and air conditioning dealers or manufacturers for ways of making your heating units safer for children.

In addition, make sure that your furniture is kept a safe distance from any heating units. This is a good safety precaution and also allows the heated air to circulate most freely and efficiently. For instance, do not have window treatments go beyond baseboard heating to the floor. Also allow for sufficient space in front of the baseboard heating so that furniture cannot block it (usually a minimum of 9").

If your child is old enough, he may enjoy finding the drafts in his room himself, and may know of some that you haven't found. If previous measures haven't solved the problem, there may be other easy solutions. Just moving a desk from a north wall (which is by nature colder than its southern counterpart) can make the difference between a happy relaxed student and a shivering, unhappy one.

Picket Fence Wallcovering Theme Matches Radiator Cover

General Lighting

Task Lighting

Shutters that Darken the Room at Nap Time

Crib that Meets Safety Standards

Dresser for Storing Clothes

Picket Fence Guards the Radiator

Toy Chest to Keep Toys Neatly Away

Easy-Care Carpet in Case of Spills and Messes

Child's Stool for Sitting

Adult Rocker for Feeding and Reading

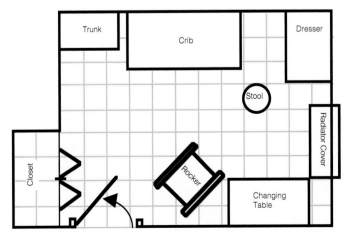

Special Activities, Special Areas

4

A s children grow, their needs and wants take on broader dimensions. Topping the list is a comfortable, properly designed place to study. With the addition of new family members, the accommodation of more than one child per room may need to be considered. Other needs may not be as obvious, and may best be answered outside of the children's room. For instance, budding athletes need areas for exercise, and even those kids that aren't good at sports need to keep physically fit. Since video is a major part of most family entertainment, setting up an area that is appropriate for kids as well as adults makes good sense. You'll want to be sure that your children take part in the planning of any special areas addressing their needs. A jointly designed area makes a child feel very special indeed.

Before you know it, kids are conversant with home computers, and you may be discussing keyboards instead of pastels, paints and crayons. In between, that same child will need a desk for drawing and writing, scaled to her own needs.

Projects you can make yourself include an easel, a modular desk and a computer center.

Setting aside special areas within a room for study, hobbies and leisure-time makes any child's room a grand place to be.

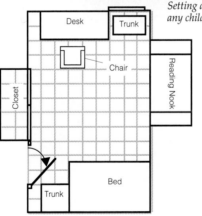

A trim desk-storage area is positioned to have a view of a unique jeep mural on the wall.

Easy Easel

As soon as they discover crayons, a delightful easel will please youngsters and can last through childhood. One side has a blackboard (with painted wood instead of slate), while the other has a drawing-pad holder. Two children can use the easel at the same time and it can be neatly folded out of the way when not in use.

Solid white oak or white oak plywood provides a natural finish, but any hardwood is suitable. Hinges at the top of the unit open the easel, while a stop latch and safety chain provide security so that young artists can't topple the unit.

You need to allow drying time for finishing as you complete various components of this project. Read over the instructions and you may find that you can take some shortcuts (for instance, you might substitute a ready-made frame). This project requires a moderate degree of skill to build, and can be put together in less than a day.

Provide a suitable environment for using the easel, especially if the artist will be using poster paints or watercolors. Position it sideways to a window so that the child is not facing into direct window light while creating his masterpieces. Allowing for both elbow room and safe spilling space, the easel should be positioned away from walls. It's best to set up the unit on a spill-resistant flooring, but if that is not possible, protect the floor with newspapers or a floorcloth. Finally, set aside a special area in your home where the artist's current works can be displayed. A bulletin board in the kitchen will encourage the creative muses.

1. Create the Blackboard and Eraser Holder. Cut the hardboard back for the blackboard to fit, and paint one side with several coats of flat black latex paint (or special blackboard paint in black or green, available in paint stores). Cut the eraser holder and its lip and round the

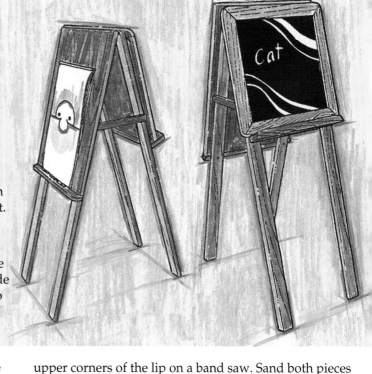

upper corners of the lip on a band saw. Sand both pieces well and finish, stain or paint as you wish.

2. Frame the Blackboard. Cut the pieces for the blackboard frame from 3/4" stock (see Blackboard Frame View, page 87). Lay the pieces roughly in position (unmitered) and lightly mark them so you can tell which is the front and which is the back side. Round the inside front edge of the frame pieces with a beading cutter in a shaper. Then use a table saw or a radial arm saw with a dado blade to cut a 1/4" x 1/4" rabbet in the inside back edges of the frame pieces (see Blackboard Frame Edge, page 87). Smooth the inside edge of the rabbet with sandpaper.

Finally, miter the pieces at a 45-degree angle at the ends to the 17$\frac{1}{2}$" length. Glue the pieces together and clamp solidly in a picture-frame clamp, checking that the frame is square. Leave to dry overnight. When dry, use miter-corner picture-frame fasteners to give the frame extra strength. Use a band saw to round the corners of the frame. Round the outside edges front and back, using a beading cutter in a shaper or router. Sand, stain or finish the frame.

3. Assemble the Blackboard. Glue the back of the blackboard into the back of the frame and use brads on each side for extra strength. Attach the lip to the

Tools & Materials

- ☐ (1) 1/4" x 14" x 14" Hardboard (For blackboard back)
- ☐ (1) 3/4" x 2$\frac{1}{2}$" x 17$\frac{1}{2}$" Hardwood Stock (For eraser holder)
- ☐ (1) 1/2" x 1$\frac{1}{2}$" x 17$\frac{1}{2}$" Hardwood Stock (For eraser holder lip)
- ☐ (4) 3/4" x 2" x 18" Hardwood Stock (For blackboard frame)
- ☐ (1) 3/4" x 17$\frac{1}{2}$" x 24" Plywood (For drawing pad holder)
- ☐ (1) 3/4" x 2" x 18" Plywood (For crayon holder)
- ☐ (4) 3/4" x 2" x 46" Hardwood Stock (For legs)
- ☐ (4) Miter Corner Picture Frame Fasteners
- ☐ Radial Arm Saw or Table Saw
- ☐ Power Shaper with Beading Cutter
- ☐ Finishing Nails
- ☐ (1) 1/2" x 3/4" x 9" Stop Latch
- ☐ (1) 14" Light Chain
- ☐ 1$\frac{1}{4}$" Wood Screws
- ☐ Small Brads
- ☐ Hammer
- ☐ Paint or Stain
- ☐ Filter Mask
- ☐ Flat Black Latex Paint
- ☐ Stain or Other Finish
- ☐ (2) 1" Butt Hinges
- ☐ Picture Frame Clamp
- ☐ (2) 1/2" Wood Screws
- ☐ Glue
- ☐ Brushes
- ☐ Safety Goggles
- ☐ Band Saw
- ☐ Screwdriver
- ☐ Sander or Sandpaper

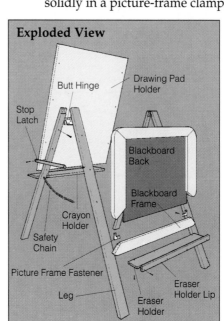

Exploded View

Stop Latch
Butt Hinge
Drawing Pad Holder
Blackboard Back
Blackboard Frame
Crayon Holder
Safety Chain
Picture Frame Fastener
Leg
Eraser Holder
Eraser Holder Lip

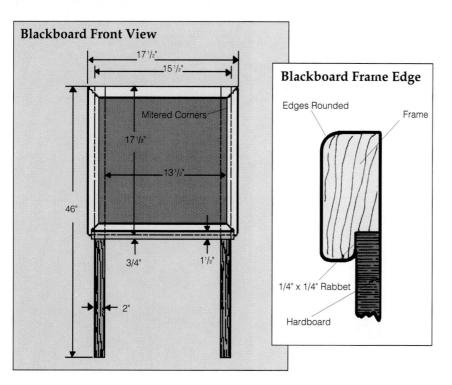

Blackboard Front View

17 1/2"
15 1/2"

Mitered Corners

17 1/2"

13 1/2"

46"

3/4"   1 1/2"

2"

Blackboard Frame Edge

Edges Rounded

Frame

1/4" x 1/4" Rabbet

Hardboard

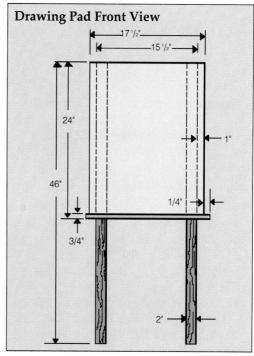

Drawing Pad Front View

17 1/2"
15 1/2"

24"

1"

46"

1/4"

3/4"

2"

eraser holder (Side View) with glue and finishing nails set below the surface. Attach the assembled eraser holder to the bottom of the blackboard frame with glue and countersunk wood screws.

4. Make the Drawing Pad Holder. Cut the drawing pad holder from a piece of hardwood-faced plywood (see Drawing Pad Front View) and sand well. You'll probably want to match the hardwood used throughout the piece. Cut the crayon holder and round the outside corners on a band saw and sand well. Apply veneer tape to finish edges of the board and crayon holder and allow the glue to dry. Finish both the pad holder and the crayon holder to match the blackboard frame. When dry, attach the crayon holder to the pad holder with glue and countersink wood screws (see Side View).

5. Cut Legs and Assemble Easel. Cut the four legs to size and round all edges with a beading cutter in a shaper. Sand the legs and finish to match other parts. When dry,

attach two of the legs to the blackboard and two to the drawing pad holder, 1" in from the edge of each (see Front Views). Use 1 1/4" wood screws, countersunk, driving them from the backs of the legs into the blackboard frame and pad holder at the top, center and bottom.

6. Finish Assembly.
Screw two 1" butt hinges to the inside edges at the tops of both pairs of legs. Cut the stop latch with a band

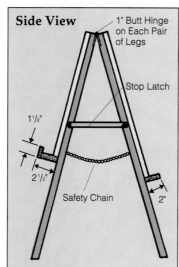

Side View

1" Butt Hinge on Each Pair of Legs

Stop Latch

1 1/2"

2 1/2"

2"

Safety Chain

saw or saber saw from 1/2" stock to the dimensions and shape (see Stop Latch). Drill a 1/4" hole in the center of the rounded end, and attach the top latch on a leg (see Side View) with a 1/4" roundhead wood screw. Drive in another roundhead wood screw directly opposite on the other leg (check exact position by marking with the stop latch in position), allowing the latch to protrude slightly more than 1/2" so the stop latch will hold onto the screw. Fasten a small brass safety chain with 1/2" screws about 3" below the stop latch to prevent the easel from falling down should the stop latch get knocked open.

7. Customize the Unit. You can lower the height of both the blackboard and drawing frame for younger children, then simply remove the screws and position these elements higher up on the easel frame as the child grows.

Install a clip on the side with the drawing board so that children can clip up sheets of any paper they want, including scrap computer paper, craft paper or whatever is at hand. You can attach a plastic cup to the easel legs to hold additional crayons or colored chalk.

By keeping the frame a neutral color, a kid's artwork becomes the major "decoration" of the unit. However, you and your child may want to decorate the easel to match the color scheme of the room, to reflect his favorite colors with matching paint (which easily can be changed), or to match wood stains of other furnishings in the room.

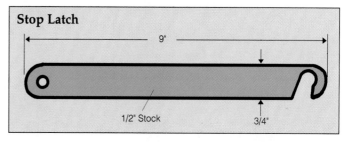

Stop Latch

9"

1/2" Stock

3/4"

Computer-Ready Modular Desk

Four components make up this hardwood desk that can be customized to suit any child's needs (it may be reconfigured to suit a corner or even made bigger if necessary). As shown, the four units include a single-drawer desk, keyboard-station desk, space for a roll-out printer and two shelving units. You can start by building just the sections your child needs, or make the entire modular unit all at once.

Check with a local computer store for the latest models of computers, to be sure that you are gearing dimensions to the electronic equipment presently available. For instance, if your child will be using a laptop computer with a pop-up screen, you may want to raise the shelving unit above the keyboard station to accommodate that height. Another option is to move the monitor down to the keyboard desktop and add a keyboard pull-out shelf. This will be a better height for a smaller child for both viewing and for using the keyboard.

Select the wood that will complement the rest of the children's room furniture or dress up the unit with paint or colorful stains.

1. Cut All Pieces. A 1" allowance has been added to all mitered edges; dimensions given reflect these additions. Adjust sizes to suit the finishing and joining technique you plan to use. Remember to cut the piece of 4' x 4' hardboard.

2. Assemble Keyboard Desk. Draw pieces on the plywood as shown and cut them out. Miter top edges of sides and backs at a 45-degree angle. Miter back edge of sides and sides of back at 45-degrees. Attach sides and back using glue and nails.

Cut two cleats from lumber, 21" long by 1" x 2" for sides. Cut back cleat 1" x 2" x 28" long to fit inside side cleats. Trim to fit, and glue and nail 4" below top edge of sides and back. Then glue and

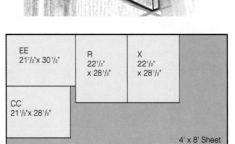

nail a face rail 1" x 2" x 32" long and trimmed to fit to the underside of the desktop, to line up with the cleats.

Apply glue to the top of the cleats and place the keyboard desk surface in position. Drive nails through the cleats and into the underside of the desk surface.

3. Assemble Drawer Desk. Cut out the pieces and miter the butting edges. Assemble the sides, back, top, using glue and nails.

Build the drawer from the 3/4" plywood and 1/4" hardboard in compliance with dimensions specified by the manufacturer of the drawer guides you select. Rabbet the drawer front and miter or butt-join back corners. Rabbet a groove 1/4" x 1/4" set 1/4 up from the bottom edge on the inside surface of sides and back to accommodate the drawer bottom. Assemble with nails and glue.

Tools & Materials

- ☐ (4) 4' x 8' Sheets of 3/4" Hardwood Plywood (Good both sides-any face veneer)
- ☐ (3) 1" x 2" x 4' Lumber
- ☐ (1) 1/4" x 4' x 4' Hardboard
- ☐ (2) Drawer Guides, 22 1/4"-Long Each
- ☐ (2) Rotating Casters, 2" Diameter
- ☐ Brush (To apply finish)   ☐ Wood Putty
- ☐ (2) Fixed Casters, 2" Diameter   ☐ Carpenter's Glue
- ☐ 8d (2 1/2") Finishing Nails   ☐ Pin-Type Shelf Clips
- ☐ Penetrating Resin Finish   ☐ (2) Drawer Handles
- ☐ Veneer Tape (To match components):
    - ☐ 8' for Keyboard Station Desk ☐ 6' for Drawer
    - ☐ 9' for Roll-Out Printer Unit ☐ 8' for Drawer Desk
    - ☐ 14' for Each Shelf Unit (28' total)
- ☐ Hack Saw (For cutting drawer guides)
- ☐ Circular Saw   ☐ Hammer
- ☐ Fine Sandpaper

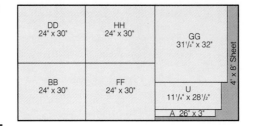

Attach the drawer guides and drawer pull (see pages 32-33 for more complete directions for building drawers). Position drawer flush to the top of the desk and place and attach the drawer guides to the inside surfaces of the desk.

4. Assemble Shelving Units. Cut out all pieces, allowing for mitered edges. Drill holes to accommodate pin-type clips per manufacturer's instructions for depth and vertical spacing. Nail and glue sides, top and bottom. Place back inside the frame flush to back edge and nail and glue into place.

5. Assemble Roll-out Printer. Refer to the illustration for construction details before cutting any pieces so you can alter the dimensions to fit the printer you have. The dimensions given are for a large printer; a smaller printer can take a smaller roll-out.

Note: The support that runs through the bottom opening is essential because it alone gives the unit rigidity and stability. Locate it so that you have plenty of room under the printer shelf for books and continuous computer paper.

Attach rails to the underside of the bottom, flush with the sides with nails and glue. Butt the bottom to the front and back, so that bottom rails are flush with the bottom edges and printer shelf is parallel to the bottom.

6. Glue and Nail. Position support in the bottom opening so that it allows paper to be fed into the back of the printer if desired (a minimum of 1/2"). Nail and glue.

Note: You can add a cleat beneath the front edge of the printer shelf if you feel it is warranted.

Install a handle on the drawer front and casters on the bottom. Note that the stationary casters belong at the back of the unit while the swivel-type casters are positioned at the front. This allows the unit to be driven under the desk for easier storage.

7. Finish All Pieces. Set all nailheads and fill the nail holes with wood putty. Glue veneer tape on all unfinished edges. Lightly sand all surfaces, including dried veneer tape. Finish as desired with penetrating resin finish, stain, paint or varnish.

Note: You may want to add a surge protector multiple outlet to the computer desk, with lines extending to the printer. You also may wish to drill a hole in the back of the computer desk to accommodate wiring for the printer.

Courtesy of Georgia-Pacific Corp.

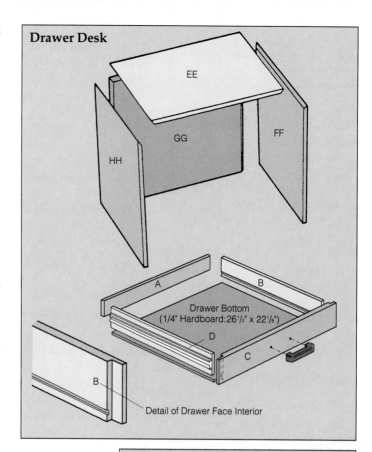

Drawer Desk

EE

GG

FF

HH

A

B

Drawer Bottom
(1/4" Hardboard:26 1/2" x 22 1/8")

D

C

B

Detail of Drawer Face Interior

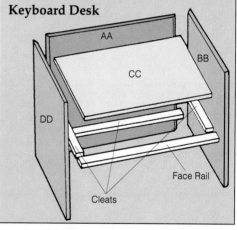

Keyboard Desk

AA

BB

CC

DD

Face Rail

Cleats

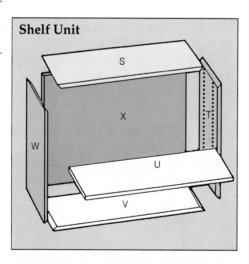

Shelf Unit

S

X

T

W

U

V

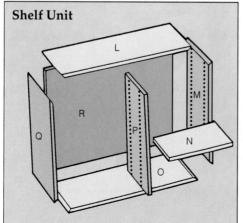

Shelf Unit

L

M

R

Q

N

O

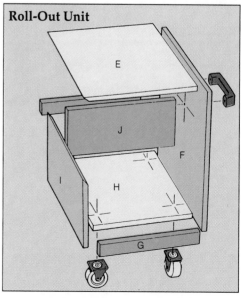

Roll-Out Unit

E

J

F

I

H

G

Video & Sound in the Children's Room

Each year brings new videos and records that can enchant and educate a child. And each year children take use of these instruments as a matter of course. Educational video tapes and even do-it-yourself productions will play an increasing role in both children's and parents lives. While some parents may opt to confine video viewing to family areas, most children will at least have a radio or a CD player of their own, in their own room, before leaving grammar school. Many will have their own televisions as well unless a playroom, designed specifically for their needs, is available.

Video Equipment

Roughhousing and serious video equipment don't mix, but can coexist if properly planned in a child's room. For toddlers, a television can be placed on a high shelf, or even a swiveling arm to keep it safe and out of the way. Remote control devices make it possible to place the television out of reach and out of danger, without becoming an inconvenience. Other alternatives are to enclose a unit in a furniture piece

or built-in. Some options include furniture such as an armoire that can be totally closed with a television set inside when not in use, or placing the set in an out of the way location that is removed from most physical activity. Or you can select a rollaway unit to hold the television, incorporating into your plans a designated spot for storing the unit during play. Make sure that electrical cords for a portable unit also are easily stored away.

When selecting a television for a child's room, there are many things to consider, including the size of the set and its placement.

Viewing the Set. Figure out where your child will most likely want to view the set. Will she be seated on his bed? Will she use a chair or seating that can be moved? Will she most likely be viewing the set from the floor? Would it make sense to have the television near her desk area? Will more than one person be viewing the television the same time? During the school-age years, children often like to view programs together. If the room is for more than one child, can seating be arranged so that both can comfortably view the set at the same time? Will you want to

Moving the television out of the way during times of play is the most practical solution in many children's rooms.

view shows or videos in the room with your child or will you have a different place to watch television?

Set Sizes. How large a set do you need? Is a portable television, which can be placed wherever it is needed, a practical solution? Is your child old enough to make sure the set is out of the way so that it poses no hazard during roughhousing?

Achieve Optimal Viewing. Use this formula as a basis for placing a television: Optimal viewing is no closer than twice the distance of the diagonal of the screen. For instance, the best approximate distance for a 12" diagonal screen would be 24". The set should be placed at a comfortable height. Ideally, the center of the screen should be at eye level or below.

Avoid Window Glare. Use the same principles for placement of a video screen as a computer terminal, eliminating lamp and daylight glare on the screen and balancing the background.

Keeping Tidy. Even children of the preschool age can help file video tapes neatly (videos often have pictures on the front that are easily identified). A storage unit that's easy to use and accessible to a child should be part of your plan.

With his own stereo system neatly stored within spacious shelves, your child will be able to listen to whatever he chooses without intruding on everyone else's quiet.

Sound Advice

If you have an infant, you'll want a sound monitor to hear virtually every breath or cry. By the time your child has discovered his own musical tastes, you'll want just the opposite—some way of isolating that sound from the rest of the house. While acoustical walls and ceilings will not totally block sound, they can go a long way in keeping the children's sounds isolated. The added benefit is

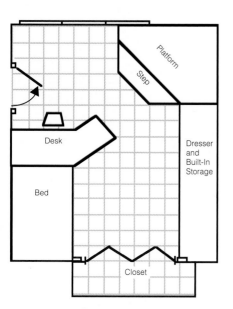

that a child also can sleep through noises baffled from the rest of the home, such as adult late-night TV viewing or parties.

Professional acoustical engineers can offer the optimum advice for soundproofing. However, if you simply want to lower the decibels a bit, there are some techniques and tips that are easy to do and require little expenditure.

Soften the Sounds. Sound-deadening carpeting and underlayment is very effective in quieting excited feet and energenic play. Combined with soft furnishings, such as curtains around the windows and fabrics on the beds, much sound gets absorbed.

Pad the Walls. Carpet-like materials used on walls can double as a bulletin board while providing sound deadening. Local home centers and building supply outlets can provide other suggestions for specific acoustic wall materials.

Add Insulation. Interior walls that are simply sheathed with sheet rock provide little resistance to sound. Add insulation to these walls. Since

electric boxes act as sound (and heat) conduits, they should be staggered (rather than placed back-to-back between rooms).

Add Acoustical Ceiling Tiles. Sound that is absorbed by ceiling tiles will not go beyond the room.

Block that Door. Hollow-core doors that transmit sound can be quieted through the addition of cork tile, fabric padding, or facing with paneling on the room's side. The sound solution is easy to convert into a decorative asset, when you incorporate the treatment into the room's decorative scheme. For instance, cover the door in a child's favorite team colors and use it for a bulletin board for game programs, banners, posters and the like.

Say No to Earphones. It is not a good idea to encourage children to use earphones in their rooms. Both children and adults tend to turn up the volume to dangerous levels. Continuous listening at high levels can cause permanent hearing loss. The danger is lessened when the sound source is from an entire room rather than directly into the ears.

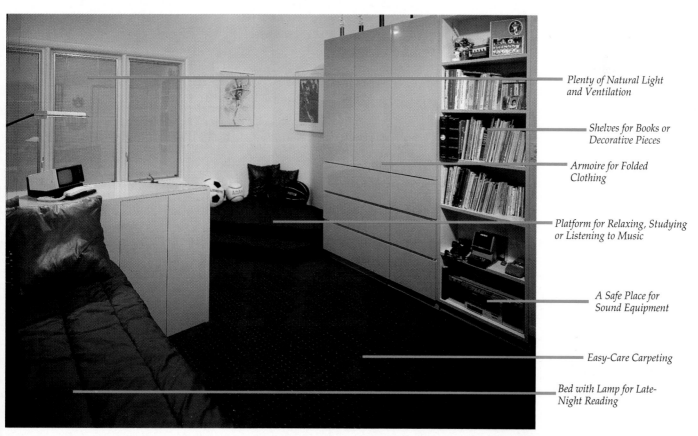

Plenty of Natural Light and Ventilation

Shelves for Books or Decorative Pieces

Armoire for Folded Clothing

Platform for Relaxing, Studying or Listening to Music

A Safe Place for Sound Equipment

Easy-Care Carpeting

Bed with Lamp for Late-Night Reading

Active Play & Exercise Areas

Kids make jungle gyms and swings out of furniture when they have no alternatives. Thankfully, simple to build tools can create active gym equipment for use in small spaces. A variety of ready-made exercise products also are available, including something that is perfect for any budding dancer, astronaut or athlete.

Exercising is a good way of dispatching excess energy. Physical activity also creates a sense of general well-being. Kids who are comfortable within their bodies and feel they have mastery over their physical movements are more likely to have positive self-images. And kids who are physically fit are far less likely to have accidents than those who are out of shape and uncoordinated.

Physical fitness experts stress that today's children spend less time exercising during the school years, partly due to changed activity schedules and partly due to an increase in sedentary pleasures such as television watching.

But kids love to exercise, given the space, time and a few simple props. With a bit of creativity the same room can be altered to grow with your child and her activity needs (see below).

Kids never get tired of climbing, sliding and hiding in this miniature jungle gym. Used indoors or out, it's a great source for playful activity.

Follow the safety rules first. Designate special areas for vigorous activity and make sure the flooring is solid and secure (rugs must be anchored down), and that there are no dangerous corners to create hazards. Let children know which areas are off-limits for exercising.

Tot-sized jungle gyms, including those with slides, are available for use indoors or out. Trampolines with handle bars for extra safety take up little room, and provide good outlets for youthful energy. The traditional hobby horse is especially good for small spaces.

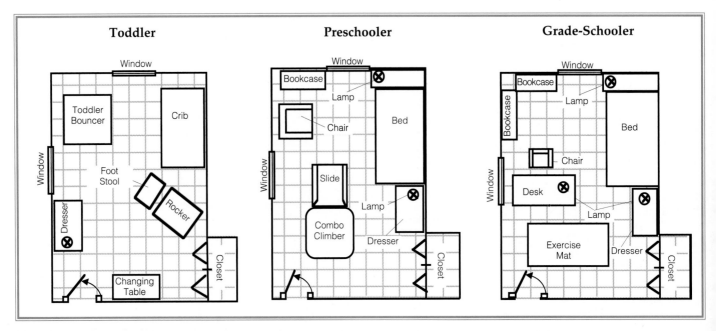

Simple Equipment

Early exercise programs with children can be built around simple equipment. A 2" x 4" x 4' placed directly on the floor, can be used to help a toddler learn balance and coordination. A balancing hand from the parent is all that's needed to make using this prop safe and fun. Hoop circles laid on a rug can form indoor hopscotch game grids, good for developing jumping skills. Painted in bright colors, these props can be permanently displayed or stored between uses.

Local nursery schools and kindergartens are good sources for simple exercise equipment ideas. Teachers also can guide parents on the appropriate materials to use at various age levels, and kinds of exercise games kids enjoy most. Exercise bars attached to the walls, for hanging or climbing, can be as simple as ladders. They should be well-sanded, finished, and positioned a few inches away from the wall itself. Make sure both the bars and the wall behind them are

A simple mat such as the one shown here is perfect for young gymnasts who like to tumble and stretch.

firm enough to withstand the exercise they will encourage.

Whether inside a child's room or in a specially outfitted playroom, exercise equipment that's available rain or shine encourages healthy activity and good, wholesome play.

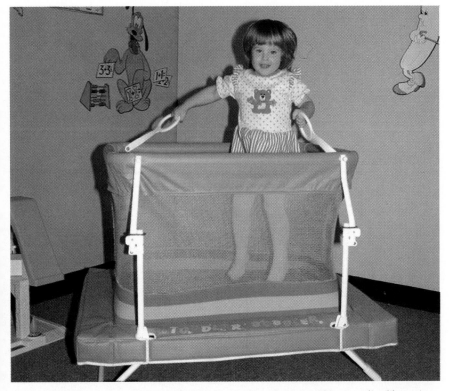

Toddlers love to jump up and down and it can be a great form of exercise. This trampoline-like toy is a safe alternative for those youngsters who may otherwise choose to jump all over couches and beds.

Sew an Exercise Mat

If the floors aren't covered with a soft material, an exercise mat is an excellent idea. The mat can perform double duty as a cushioned seating area for other, more quiet floor-based activities. You can make one yourself by taking a 2" piece of firm foam and covering it with poplin or canvas. Sew a large envelope to encase the mat, which should be at least 5' long (to accommodate summersaults) and 24" to 30" wide.

Allow at least 3/4" hem to border the mat. Cut two lengths for the cover, one for the top and one for the bottom (they do not need to be the same fabric). Place the front and back pieces (outer sides) together, and stitch around three sides and partway across one end. Turn right-side out and insert the foam mat. Top-stitch the opening at the end. Add tabs to tie the mat about 6" in from the sides at one end, and long enough to encircle the mat when rolled for storage.

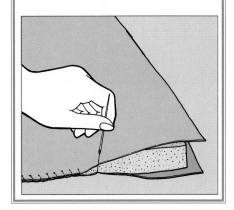

Rocking Horse

This rocker is for the middle-sized riders. Measure your child to see if his feet will reach the platform. Take extra care to cut and sand the rockers to ensure the smoothest rocking action. This project should be sanded until very smooth; it will get a lot of use from bare legs. Paint the horse's head, body, and legs, then decorate with bright colors.

1. Cut the Parts. Enlarge the squared drawing of the head (see Head) and transfer the pattern to a piece of 3/4"

plywood. Cut out the head with a band saw, coping saw or saber saw, drill a 1/2" hole where indicated, and sand the head smooth rounding the edges with sandpaper.

Enlarge the squared drawings for the two sides and the spacer (see Body), the four legs (see Leg), the four wedges (see Leg Wedge), the two rockers (see Rocker), and the seat (see Seat). Cut out all the pieces from 1" x 12" clear pine or other suitable stock. Cut the two platform pieces to the given dimensions (see Platform, page 95). Sand these pieces, except the wedges, and round the top edge of the seat with a rasp.

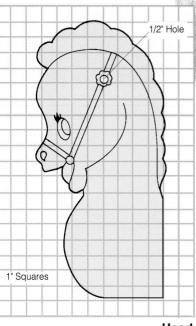

Head

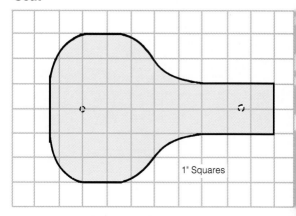

1" Squares

Body Spacer
(Cut 1)

Position of Front Leg Position of Back Leg

Body Side
(Cut 2)

Body

1" Squares

(Cut 2)

Rocker

Leg

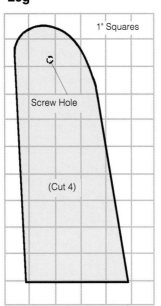

1" Squares

Screw Hole

(Cut 4)

(Cut 4)

Cross Section of Wedge

1" Squares

Leg Wedge

Seat

1" Squares

2. Assemble the Body. Lay one side piece down (out-side down) on a flat surface, coat it with carpenter's glue, and seat the spacer and head on it making sure that all edges are flush (see Exploded View). Coat the inside of the other side piece with glue and seat it on the head and spacer so that all edges are flush; clamp the assembly with C-clamps. Wipe away any glue that squeezes out and allow to dry.

3. Attach the Legs. Use the enlarged squared drawing of the sides (see Body, page 94) to mark the position of the legs on the body. Glue the wedges to the tops of the legs (be sure they are on the inside of the legs), clamp, and allow to dry. When dry, drill 3/16" hole and countersink in the legs, as indicated (see Leg, page 94). Attach the legs to the body, as shown, with glue and No. 10 x 1³/₄" flathead wood screws.

4. Attach the Body. Mark the position of the legs on the platform pieces (see Platform), with the outside edge of each leg 2¹/₂" from the edge of the platform. Drill and countersink two 3/16" holes in the platform in each position where the legs attach; fasten the platforms to the legs with glue and No. 10 x 1¹/₂" flathead wood screws. Drill and countersink two 3/16" holes at the ends of the platform pieces and attach the platforms to the rockers with glue and No. 10 x 1¹/₂" flathead wood screws.

5. Finish the Rocking Horse.
Drill and countersink two 3/16" holes in the seat (see Seat, page 94), and attach the seat to the body with glue and No. 10 x 1¹/₂" wood screws driven into the spacer. Drill a 3/8" hole about 3/4" deep in the center of the spacer at the back, just below the seat, and glue in a 5" or 6" rope or yarn tail. Cover all the countersunk screw heads with wood putty, allow to dry, and touch up with paint. Finally, cut a 6" length of 1/2" dowel and glue it, centered, in the hole in the head; this will serve as a handle. Paint on the facial features, as shown in the squared drawing and add detail to the body (see Exploded View).

Courtesy of U-Bild Newspaper Syndicate

Exploded View

Platform

Tools & Materials

- ☐ (1) 3/4" x 15" x 18" Plywood (For the head)
- ☐ (2) 3/4" x 6³/₄" x 16¹/₂" Plywood (For the sides)
- ☐ (1) 3/4" x 6" x 1" Plywood (For the spacer)
- ☐ (4) 3/4" x 4¹/₂" x 9³/₄" Solid Stock (For the legs)
- ☐ (2) 3/4" x 3¹/₄" x 5¹/₄" Solid Stock (For wedges)
- ☐ (1) 3/4" x 6¹/₄" x 9³/₄" Plywood or Solid Stock (For the seat)
- ☐ (2) 1" x 3⁷/₈" x 12" Plywood or Solid Stock (For the platforms)
- ☐ (1) 1/2" x 6" Dowel (For the handle)
- ☐ No. 10 x 1³/₄" Flathead Wood Screws
- ☐ No. 10 x 1¹/₂" Flathead Wood Screws
- ☐ Paint
- ☐ Band Saw, Coping Saw or Saber Saw
- ☐ (1) Short Piece of Rope   ☐ Glue
- ☐ Wood Putty   ☐ Drill
- ☐ Rasp   ☐ Screwdriver
- ☐ Sander or Sandpaper   ☐ C-Clamps

Satisfying Shared Rooms

When it comes to sharing rooms, one plus one can equal armed warfare unless properly planned. Shared space and equally important private areas are necessary to preserve the peace. Size isn't as important as organized functioning paired with an understanding of the personalities and needs of those sharing the space.

During the early years, a shared play area can totally dominate a room. Provisions must be made, however, for one child to sleep while the other is quietly active. Some method of blocking off a child's bed (not necessarily completely), becomes almost essential when a child is ill and needs soothing quiet. Doubled storage space for both clothes and toys also helps in sharing the spoils.

By the time children enter school, if not before, each child needs a quiet area for reading and studying, separate from her sibling. Individual study habits can vary greatly from child to child, as can the length and involvement of each in her work or hobbies. As a child differentiates herself and develops her own interests, her needs for reserved spaces, where she is totally in control, becomes an important ingredient to developing a good sense of herself. Both children benefit from having clearly defined areas where the other child cannot play or use things without asking her roommate first.

The problems are in some ways harder when children separated by a few years share the same space, since the younger child may not understand (or honor) the older child's property rights. Here, physical walls or half-walls make it easier for the younger child to respect the older child's wishes. On the other hand, a few years age difference generally means that there will be less competition among the siblings and the older child usually has more patience with a younger, helping to establish and maintain limits where needed.

Shared interests such as playing with dolls may make it possible to allocate shared space, as in this wide-open room.

Sometimes the best way of setting up a shared room is to have totally equal allocations of space and identical furnishings.

Visual Separations

The use of visual separations is extremely important in dividing children's rooms.

■ Place heads of beds so that kids are looking away from each other, not towards one another.

■ Use roll-down shades to provide privacy for naps or sleep. Shades or drawn curtains are easy to add to bunk beds and have all the charm of old-fashioned railroad pullman beds, or instant puppet stages for play.

■ Make sure that lighting (especially for bedtime reading) is confined to each child's area without cascading onto the other child.

■ Use color to identify each child's belongings and areas. Have each child select a favorite color, then develop a scheme utilizing both colors. Use a common print or a third color to bridge the two; for instance, use an Indian blanket pattern with turquoise, terra cotta and beige on both beds. Furniture and sheets for one child can be turquoise, and for the other, terra cotta.

Primary colors are classic "keys" to divide up possessions and furniture among children. Don't feel you have to use a total dose of the color; trim on woodgrained or neutral beige, grey or white furniture provides sufficient visual change of pace.

■ If both children love the same color, go into reverse to separate the areas. For instance, if the scheme is blue and white, use white polka dots on blue for one child and blue polka dots on white for the other. Perfect for this sort of idea, many fabrics are available in reverse colorations.

■ Use mirrors in children's rooms to make them appear larger. Mirrors also can be used to create the impression of a window in an area that has none.

■ Remember that most kids love cozy cubbyholes; what may seem cramped to you may be just the right scale and size to a small child.

■ Use visual tricks to compensate for breaking a large area into small vertical areas. By making an area

A bunk bed unit that arranges beds in an "L" plus another bed all fit into limited space efficiently in this room. Hand-painted walls add interest without taking up space.

smaller, you automatically make the ceiling seem higher. To lower the look, extend paint or wallcovering up to plate rail height (about 12" below the ceiling). Then paint above that in a tone that matches the ceiling or use a border. Consider using wallcovering with horizontal stripes to make the room seem less high and wider.

■ Invest in the most adaptable furniture, window treatments and carpets. With two personalities in the same room, you may want to change looks more often than you would with only one child.

■ Children of different ages outgrow age-specific motifs at different times, so stick with classic patterns.

■ Plan space for private expressive areas. Posters, ribbons, school banners may be treasured by one child, while revolting to the other! Create areas where these things can be displayed to the child who loves them, without affecting the rest of the room. For instance, face a bulletin board away from the center of the room.

■ Create individual shelf display areas. Special treasures such as train models and miniature dolls help personalize each child's area.

■ Provide each child with his own book and homework areas. This can be as simple as assigning separate shelves in a single unit or as specific as entirely separate bookcases. Each child needs his own desk.

Equal spaces for sleeping and studying provide the necessary private space, as does placement of the beds so that children face away from each other in this room.

Divvying Up the Space

There are ways to physically meld two children into one area. Making over the room may be as dramatic as creating two rooms from the one, or as simple as using visual tricks to set off the two areas. Some of the suggestions are ideal for setting up a single child's room to accommodate the occasional overnight guest.

Begin by defining your children's needs. List the obvious, such as: sleeping, study, clothes storage, toy storage, play space, artwork and wall display spaces. You and each child can fill in details of what's important for each area. For instance, under sleeping, you can list a lamp for reading in bed, extra space for stuffed animals, and space to provide for easy, do-it-yourself bedmaking. To avoid constant rearranging, anticipate for future needs and work them into your design now.

In most cases, kids can share some of the spaces needed. Play space and TV viewing space, exercising areas and hobby tables often are accommodating to overlapping needs. Something like an aquarium or special wall decoration should be planned so that it is equally available to both children.

Separating a girl and boy in the same room becomes easy with this unique storage wall.

Furniture Dividers. One solution for dividing a room is to invest in the type of furniture that creates cubes that incorporate study, sleeping and storage all within a freestanding unit. Often, two sides in a freestanding cube arrangement are used exclusively by one child, while the remaining two sides of the cube serves the other child. Bunks at different levels accommodate each child. Similar units are designed in an "L" arrangement to fit flush to wall. You can use freestanding bookcases to create functional room dividers. Bookcases with finished backs will allow you to reverse them, some facing into one child's area and others facing the other child's area. The backs can be used as bulletin boards. Armoires and wardrobes can be placed with great effect back-to-back or staggered as room dividers.

For added safety, you can anchor furniture, using L-brackets, to either the floor or ceiling. Another method is to use a spring pole from the top of the unit twisted taut to the ceiling.

The partition wall is reversed on the other side to provide a bulletin board space and storage for the other child.

A decidedly feminine tack is taken in this section (above left), adding pinks to the basic scheme. Extra storage beneath a captain's bed and green and white checks give this section (above right) an entirely different look.

Half Walls. When creating two separate rooms isn't practical, other alternatives that are almost as effective are readily at hand. It is critical to enlist both children in the decision-making process as to how spaces can be shared and what decorations should be used.
You can negotiate these matters, but having the children agree to the arrangement from the beginning is the best way of making sure they will be happy with the results. Even so, you will want to take advantage of all the tricks you can use to create a sense of physical separation.

One good way of delineating space is by using a half-wall. Often constructed at wainscot level, 30" or 40" high, half-walls provide privacy for children while seated or lying in bed, and at the same time allow for good air and light circulation throughout both sides of the room. Horizontal divisions through half-walls allow you to build in storage while you create the divider.

Another divider can be created vertically instead of horizontally. In this case, a screen, blind, floating panel or hanging banner can be used to form separate cubicles out of one large space.

Be sure all temporary dividers are adequately anchored to the floor or ceiling so they won't tip over.

Partition Walls. Having a good storage system, with furniture that is highly functional, is the key to making two working rooms out of one space. An ingenious closet storage system that doubles space efficiency can be used to eliminate freestanding furniture. This solution may well be the best for older children who want complete privacy.

Before deciding to build a partition wall, there are many things you should consider. First of all, be sure that you have allocated enough space for traffic around furnisings so that the rooms will not be cramped. Note the placement of windows and electrical outlets; they should be workable in each of the "new" rooms. Air circulation and heating

efficiency also will be affected, although fans and vents can often overcome many problems.

You can even give the wall sound-barrier qualities by employing acoustical tricks. Insulation in the wall plus staggering the studs helps eliminate sound carrying from one room to another. Materials used to cover the wall also add to its sound-deadening properties. Good choices include: padding covered with fabric, acoustical tiles, or fabric simulating carpeting designed specifically for its sound dispersing qualities.

Be aware that over time, you may need to renegotiate the space that you have divided. For instance, the common play space that works for preschoolers may best be divided for school-age children who need larger work and study areas. As your children's interests grow and change, so will the best division of their space.

Step-by-step directions for building partition walls can be found in the book, *Walls, Floors & Ceilings* published by Creative Homeowner Press.

A compact closet system with front dresser-like units that slide sidewise on tracks to reveal hanging clothes can be used back-to-back to make two rooms out of one, each a mirror image of the other. The same wall holds a cubicle for a desk.

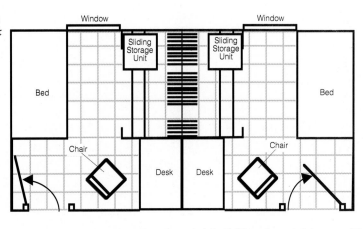

Throughout the House

Parents agree, having children changes the very basic concepts of a home's uses and good design. Kids aren't confined to their rooms and parents want to share time with them in other parts of the home as well. In many homes, small bedrooms dictate that another large play space or a series of small ones are needed for everyday children's activities.

All of the safety precautions mentioned for a child's room relate to the rest of the house as well. Childproofing a living room, dining area and even master bedroom and bath are prudent from the moment that a baby becomes a toddler.

There are special areas that deserve more thoughtful designing for the specific use of children. Among these are the bathroom, kitchen and playrooms. Each has its own special adaptations for use by kids.

Kids' artwork decorates the walls of this eat-in area of the kitchen (above), while the great plains of the Southwest adorn a storage wall in a spacious living area (far left). A decorating style that includes the children lets them know that they are an important part of the family.

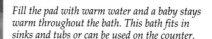

Fill the pad with warm water and a baby stays warm throughout the bath. This bath fits in sinks and tubs or can be used on the counter.

Baths
from Baby On Up

Bathing is a key part of every child's life, making the bathroom a very important environment. Those designed around a child's smaller size enable him to move most effortlessly into taking charge of his own personal hygiene.

If adults and children share a bathroom, take whatever steps seem prudent to design a safe bath. It is easy for adults to accommodate to the smaller scale (and lower levels) that are appropriate for kids. In most newer homes, a second bath has been added to the plans, leading the way for the "children only" bath.

Infants and Toddlers. Organize the bathroom around your needs for bathing the child. You'll want everything you will need right at hand so you can keep a constant vigil on the baby; keep in mind that a child can drown in less than 2" of water in a baby tub or unlocked toilet, even a bucket filled with water.

Appropriate furnishings include a comfortable seating area for drying the baby or toweling a toddler, a

What child wouldn't love a tub shaped like this? The tub itself is made of soft material, while the shower behind the glass blocks is constructed of ceramic tiles with matching non-skid tiles on the floor.

convenient place to put a baby bath, and ample storage for shampoos, talcs, wash cloths, towels, diapers, toys, a hamper and diaper pail.

Consider your own comfort in positioning a baby bath. Counter height probably will be most comfortable, or you may want to consider a freestanding bathing unit.

This double sink is so colorful it makes hygiene fun. Note the rounded edges of the counter, and hidden locking latches on the base cabinets that are designed to thwart toddlers.

Take the time to set the hot water below 120° F to prevent scalding (it still may be uncomfortably hot). A child can be scalded within 3 seconds, his skin is so much thinner and more tender than adult skin.

As far as fixtures go, a number of special advances include a pressure balancing feature which maintains the same degree of hotness even when cold water flow is reduced (such as by flushing a toilet). Single-handled fittings are easier for a child to regulate than double ones that call for hand-mixing of cold and hot water. Available now are double levers that can be preset at a desired temperature whenever turned on.

Hand-held showers can be retrofitted onto conventional shower outlets if needed. You'll use the shower head at its lower level to rinse a toddler. When the child grows, he can use the lowered shower head without assistance.

Tubs can be made safer for children for very little money. There are special soft covers for faucets so that children will not be hurt if they bump into them. Tub floors can be treated with both anti-slipping decals and mats, and lower grab bars can help children gain a grip, especially in getting in and out of the tub. One manufacturer even produces a tub that a child can walk into. Another produces a soft tub made of a squishy foam with a waterproof surface to soften falls. For the parent, there are mats that extend over the tub side, cushioning the arms of the adult holding a child. Part of the mat rests on the floor to pad adult knees.

Simple conveniences you can build include safe storage for washing materials that move easily where you need them. Add to this a basket to hold bath toys.

It is a good idea to use easy-care wallcoverings and flooring. From the first moment a toddler learns to splash, any claims to toughness are tested. Classic selections include tiles, waterproof wallcoverings, gloss and semigloss paints. Panel sheets, designed with vinyl or other water-resistant surfaces are now available.

If you are considering a major remodeling job at this point, there are a variety of fixtures which provide more efficient use of space. Since many "family" bathrooms still average under 6' x 10', you'll want to remodel efficiently.

Lower, one-piece toilets that hug closer to the wall and are longer and narrower in the seat make toilet training a little easier. Standing at about 20" high instead of the conventional 24", they are scaled better for children and are just as convenient for adults.

Preschoolers. Toilet training and the beginning of self-grooming mark this stage, necessitating a few changes in the way the child will use the bathroom. Tubs and toys seem to go together here. You'll need more room for toy storage—gear it to something the child can access himself. And plan a safe harbor for the step-stool which is essential to a preschooler's use of the toilet and sink. Consider installing a platform in front of the sink, or perhaps lower the sink down to 31" to accommodate his size.

Since vanity mirrors should be placed 8" above the counter surface to avoid splatters, you'll need to provide special mirrors for fledgling

groomers. A standing mirror or one that extends from the wall at a child's height solves this problem. Towel racks placed at the proper height are equally important. Allow at least 24" of hanging depth for full-size towels.

Grade-Schoolers. Socializing skills in school reinforce the needs for individual identity at home, including very specific grooming styles as a child gets older. Storage areas once devoted to bathtub toys may now be taken over with grooming aids. Even so, banish electric appliances such as hair dryers to another room until children are mature enough to understand the danger of electric appliances and water.

Shared Spaces. The crunch starts when kids begin fledgling toilet training, and continues through years of mornings spent preparing for school.

To cope with the increased demands, create private areas within the bath. First, make sure that a half-bath can't be squeezed out of some area. If not, move activities, such as dressing and grooming, into each child's room.

Partitioning off the bath itself is a sensible solution if it must be shared.

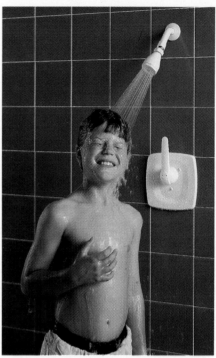

Safety features for this special shower system include a temperature range setting and equalizer no matter what the water pressure.

Enclosing the water closet and the tub will allow one child to use the sink area while another privately uses other areas. If possible, try to fit in separate sinks. Smart use of storage space and color-keyed towels and accessories can clearly show what belongs to whom in shared spaces.

Bathroom Safety

Tub & Shower Areas
- Safety glazing
- Doors hinged to prevent pinched fingers
- Grab bars at two levels: adult and child
- Shower seat

Water Closet
- Locked lids for younger children
- A lower level (on some newer models)
- Tip-resistant training step-stool
- Toilet paper within child's reach

Plumbing
- Tub valve placements within easy reach
- Single-control valves for scald prevention
- Pressure and temperature limiting valves
- Adjustable, sliding hand-shower

Electrical
- Ground fault circuit interrupter circuitry
- Sliding or covered receptacles
- Vapor-proof light fixtures
- Low voltage task lighting
- Outlets placed away from water
- Night-light, smoke detector and intercom

Cabinetry & Counter Surfaces
- Maximum 8" depth for cabinets over toilet
- Small doors, easily opened
- Childproof locks
- Rounded corners and edges
- Seating for putting on clothes

Flooring
- Slip resistant surface
- Water-resistant, easy care
- No throw rugs (unless anchored)

Windows & Doors
- Doors that swing out
- Door locks that can be opened outside
- Windows with safety bars
- Windows accessible for easy opening

This list is based on one developed by the national "Safe Bath" project as part of the National Safe Kids Campaign. For more information, call 1-900-466-SAFE; it's $2.95 per call.

Charming cows decorate the streamlined kitchen with counter seating.

Kitchens & Keeping Rooms

Kids and kitchens have gone together since Colonial times. Often, a baby's first view of the world was from the "keeping room"—a special area beside the kitchen. Used as a nursery for newborns, this room could be kept warm and was within a mother's sight while she went about her cooking chores.

The kitchen still remains a common meeting place for parents and kids to this day, although now a grade-schooler may be fixing the meals for the family in the microwave!

Infants and Toddlers. During the toddler years safety comes first. Invest in childproof, locked cabinets and scald-preventing safety rims to use on ranges. Kids can get into the kitchen quickly, making these and similar precautions a good idea. Confining a child in a play yard or playpen while you cook is obviously the best idea. Consider your kitchen layout and place a playpen in an area away from the normal traffic patterns. For instance, you may want to place it within a dining room that has a clear view of the kitchen so you can watch a child while you cook and

he can be comforted by seeing you while he plays.

Keeping rooms took into account the needs of nursing mothers. Often, a bed was moved into the room and mother and baby stayed right there, particularly a baby born in the cold winter months.

Some aspects of an old-fashioned keeping room can be found in today's modern kitchens. For instance, it is important to provide a comfortable area for a mother of an

infant. A soft chair or rocker for feeding and cuddling will prove invaluable. A seat for the baby, away from the cooking area, will enable mom to heat formula or food while baby is safely out of mother's arms.

Since a toddler's dining habits are traditionally messy, opt for easy-care materials around the space where a high chair will be, and also around a table where you may be feeding an infant. Resilient or stain-resistant wood floors are good choices, making cleanups easy. Vinyl wallcoverings or paneling and stain-resistant paint are ideal in this situation. Select your kitchen furniture with stain resistance as well; no fancy fabrics here.

Preschoolers. Most parents find that meals with preschoolers are largely kitchen bound. Booster seats can adapt chairs to fit a child's smaller size in a breakfast area, as can the use of pillows in a banquette arrangement.

In addition to regular meals, kids this age need a convenient place to have frequent snacks. Many kitchens have an area where a small snack counter can be added. Room for one or two is all that's probably needed, and a depth of a mere 12" is sufficient for a snack of a beverage plus a sandwich or cookies. If such a counter faces into a wall, use decorating tricks to add whimsy and charm. Decorative tiles or

A charming Great Room features a fireplace integrated into a mural on the wall, with the mantle acting as the wagon's back and firescreen below completing the illusion.

wallcovering borders judiciously placed as a splash plate behind the counter add interest and make spills easy to clean up. Bring in a view by placing a strip of mirrors above the splash plate, and complete the effect with colorful placemats and convivial lighting.

Other counter options include visually integrated extensions of the kitchen area. Often, family room extensions allow for the easy placement of a counter that faces into the kitchen. While kitchen-height counters are comfortable for adult snacking, usually they are not comfortable for kids. High stools can be insurmountable obstacles for a child to position and then climb aboard.

A wonderful solution for a children's eating bar is a step-down counter extension. The side with the chairs is lowered to conventional table height, while the kitchen side of the counter remains at the conventional kitchen height. In addition, a raised "barrier" can be added to keep food preparation items visually separated from where kids eat.

A barrier is more attractive from an adjacent eating area or playroom. Another option is to extend a table that's child height (even a flea market find that's been cut down to size) from the counter.

Chairs of the normal height, especially those with foot rails, swivel seats and substantial heft, are most convenient for adults and children in a counter arrangement. Resist stools that have no backs, unless you need to store them under the counter when not in use.

Grade-Schoolers. Kids take on the preparation of their own snacks and even meals as they get older. Reevaluate the food preparation area so that a child can have an area of her own that is out of the way of your fixing main meals. A simple shifting of favorite snacks such as peanut butter and jelly with crackers, along with small plates and napkins all consolidated in one area, will allow a child to prepare her own snacks.

Kitchen Safety

- Electric outlets MUST close off.
- Conceal appliance cords so they cannot be pulled by children.
- Store appliances out of the way and unplugged when not in use (consider covered "garage" ports on countertops).
- Select appliances with controls and knobs above a toddler's reach, for example, a range top with knobs on the top rather than on the front.
- Recess cooktops away from the edge of the counter so children cannot reach knobs or hot surfaces.
- Retrofit appliances with devices that provide safety (install a guard rail for the front of range tops).
- Latch refrigerators, freezers, washers or cabinets that a child could become trapped within.
- Keep hot foods out of the reach of children. Pivot the handles of glasses or pots and pans away from the edge of countertops. Do not handle hot beverages while holding a baby.
- Install safety stops on cabinet doors and drawers so that children's fingers are protected from getting caught.
- Make sure that cabinet knobs are large enough so that, if a child is able to remove one, he cannot choke on it.
- Check all surfaces for dangerous heat levels, especially ovens. Select an oven with a double insulated door that won't heat to burning, or cover it with an insulation pad. You can make one with fire resistant fabric that can be attached to the oven door handle or directly to the oven with Velcro.
- Make sure a fire extinguisher is handy and in working condition.
- A kitchen smoke detector is a must.
- Keep potentially lethal products under lock and key. Included are cleansers, plastic bags, light bulbs, some foods, liquor and sharp utensils.
- Don't place irresistible objects on counters. For instance, an animal-shape cookie jar may encourage a child to climb up to it.
- Select rounded countertop edges (bullnose shapes are readily available).
- Select base cabinets with rounded corners or add corner guards while children are young.

Lunch boxes and utensils a child needs can be consolidated in the same space.

From the moment children are old enough to create their own artwork, it traditionally is showcased in the kitchen. While the proverbial refrigerator doors with magnets holding artwork and momentos are great catchalls, most kids would be delighted with a specific display area in the kitchen. You can combine a simple corkboard or metallic board with a message center, to serve as the family check-in station.

While not every kitchen has room for a kid's eating counter, many do have space for a breakfast nook or kitchen table. To make this furniture more child-friendly, bolster them with additional seat and back pillows until kids grow into adult-sized chairs. It's unfair to expect kids not to fidget if they are uncomfortably seated.

If yours is a family that enjoys mealtime discussions, consider adding a reference book section. A dictionary and atlas are good starter books, along with bird identification guides if you and the kids are fortunate enough to have a feeder nearby the kitchen windows.

While at some point most kids will want to go to their own rooms or outside to relax and play after school, young kids may want to stay in the center of things by using the kitchen table for homework and other sedentary projects. If this is the case in your home, make sure that lighting is adequate to the task.

It's a far cry from the kitchen kept warm by hours of fireplace cooking to the modern-day variation where "nuking" of popcorn takes place in seconds. But the kitchen remains the main room of the house for most of us, certainly a center of comfort for most children.

If you're lucky enough to have space to devote entirely to child's play, decorate it accordingly with easy-care surfaces such as this Colorforms wallcovering.

Playrooms Everywhere

Family rooms off the kitchen convert readily to combination adult and child play spaces. And they often are the easiest areas to devote primarily to children. You also can convert a living room to a playroom with adult accommodations melded in, if space limitations demand it. Such short-term solutions may be the best idea in a small house with many kids, or during the early ages when children shouldn't be left unsupervised. Many spaces in the home have the potential to be play spaces and should not be overlooked. Kids don't always need large areas.

Great Rooms & Family Rooms

Unlike the confined spaces of old, contemporary homes and those remodeled to reflect modern needs often encompass a "Great Room" extension to the kitchen. Designed as a family gathering place, it enables the family to be together during meal preparation. It also provides an informal surrounding where children and adults alike need not be worried about formality. This room provides the perfect setting for showcasing trophies bestowed to youthful competitors (see Trophy/Model Case Project, page 110). While each family, as a group,

will want to decide what elements to include in their Great Room there are certain decorating criteria you will want to incorporate (the choices may vary as kids grow through different life stages).

Comfortable Seating. Here's the perfect spot for plush upholstered pieces that invite lounging, and chairs that can be pulled up to create conversational groupings or moved into alignment for viewing a cozy fire or movie on the VCR. Ample pillows can make it more comfortable for children. Contemporary sofas often have lower seating decks which are easier for children to climb onto.

The Upholstered Furniture Action Council (UFAC), founded in 1974, has created a voluntary standard of its manufacturer members for construction that is more resistant to smoldering cigarettes (and other fire sources) than other upholstered furniture. It makes sense that any furniture used near a kitchen area should be as safe as possible. Today, over 90 percent of upholstered furniture is made according to UFAC construction criteria, and can be identified by a hang tag the UFAC emblem printed on it. Over 90 percent

of cigarettes tested on the furniture with this standard by the Consumer Product Safety Commission extinguished without igniting the furniture.

Stain resistance and easy-care fabrics used on upholstery are convenience features you'll want to have as well. Even some of the sumptuous glove-like leathers and their imitators are remarkably easy to keep clean.

While adult seating doubles for children's seating, consider establishing a special section for kids as well. Small upholstered pieces (including inexpensive units that fold out into mattresses), might be better choices for preschoolers. Whimsical shapes in foam, covered with fabrics, can be playscape sculptures that double for lounging or seating in a Great Room.

Activity Center. A game table for adults and older children can perform many functions. Crosswords, card games, board games and crafting are all shared activities that can be centered around a game table. Look for durable surfaces on a game table, upholstered seats (and sometimes backs) on chairs, wheels for rolling around, and other comfort and convenience feature such as swiveling and tilting.

Wall systems incorporating home theater viewing screens of substantial size and state of the art sound systems provide family entertainment.

Playroom Table & Chair Set

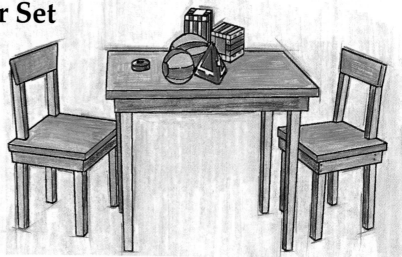

Preschoolers and even those into early school years will appreciate having their own table and chair set, scaled for them. Here's one you can make yourself, gearing it to the design of your family room.

Child-scaled furniture from the playroom or playhouse has a charm that transcends the decades. Anyone lucky enough to have her own child's furniture to pass along to the next generation is sharing a tradition that will continue for years. And if family children's furniture isn't readily available, any made now will surely become future heirlooms.

Moderate skills and workshop tools are required to complete this set, which will not take more than a day to complete. The design of this table and chair set is sufficiently simple that it lends itself to personalizing. For instance, you can paint the set in your child's favorite colors, decorate it with alphabet and number stencils, select favorite motifs from nursery rhymes, paint impressionistic plates, cups and saucers on the tabletop, or just use simple patterns of geometric stripes, checks and circles.

Don't overlook the chairs. Numbers and letters decorating the backs and seats, even allover floral stencils and vines are fun to do. You can further personalize the design by varying the shape and size of the chair backs and table aprons without altering the proportions that are designed into the set. Tooling and adding other woodworking details and your selection of wood will make this project unique to your family and kids.

Tools & Materials

Table:
- ☐ (1) 3/4" x 22" x 30" Plywood (For tabletop)
- ☐ (1) 22" x 30" Plastic Laminate (For top)
- ☐ (2) 3/8" x 1" x 23" (For top trim)
- ☐ (2) 3/8" x 1" x 31" (For top trim)
- ☐ (2) 3/4" x 2 3/8" x 18 1/2" (For apron)
- ☐ (2) 3/4" x 2 3/8" x 21 1/2" (For apron)
- ☐ (4) 1 1/2" x 1 1/2" x 21 1/2" (For legs)
- ☐ (4) 3/4" x 1 1/2" x 6" (For leg braces)
- ☐ (4) Splines (For apron)
- ☐ Top Fasteners with Screws
- ☐ 3/4" Brads
- ☐ Plastic Laminate Adhesive

Two Chairs:
- ☐ No. 8 x 1 1/2" Roundhead Brass Wood Screws
- ☐ No. 8 x 1 1/2" Flathead Wood Screws
- ☐ (8) 1 1/2" x 1 1/2" x 11 3/4" Solid Stock (For legs)
- ☐ (4) 3/4" x 2" x 10 1/2" (For front and back aprons)
- ☐ (4) 3/4" x 2" x 12" (For side aprons)
- ☐ (2) 3/4" x 13" x 13" (For seatboards)
- ☐ (4) 1 1/4" x 1 1/4" x 10" (Back supports)
- ☐ (2) 3/4" x 3 1/2" x 13" (For backs)
- ☐ 1 1/2" x 3/8" Dowels
- ☐ (8) 3/4" x 1 1/2" x 6" (For leg braces)
- ☐ (4) 5/8" x 4" Dowels

For Both Projects:
- ☐ No. 8 x 1 1/2" Roundhead Wood Screws
- ☐ Table Saw or Radial Arm Saw
- ☐ Jointer or Plane
- ☐ Router
- ☐ Doweling Jig
- ☐ Clamps and Bar Clamps
- ☐ Sander or Sandpaper
- ☐ Stain or Other Finish
- ☐ Band Saw
- ☐ Drill or Drill Press
- ☐ Glue
- ☐ Screwdriver
- ☐ Safety Goggles and Filter Mask

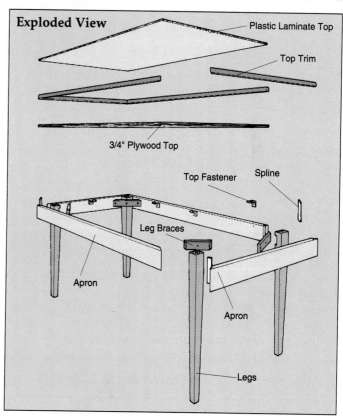

Exploded View

Plastic Laminate Top

Top Trim

3/4" Plywood Top

Top Fastener

Spline

Leg Braces

Apron

Apron

Legs

When this project is complete, be sure to sign and date it. Family pieces such as these take on even more meaning when the history is indelibly imprinted upon them.

This set is designed to fit children from about 2 years old through grade-school age, and is sturdily constructed for the many (often unlikely) uses to which it will be put. The set also is excellent for providing extra seating for meals or snacks. After making the original two chairs, you may want to make two more to accommodate your children's playmates.

Any hardwood is suitable for this design, including oak, maple or walnut. Making the top of easy-to-clean plastic laminate will enable kids to play without worrying about damaging your creation. Apply the laminate yourself or purchase ready-made 3/4" countertop.

The Table

1. Make the Tabletop. Cut a piece of the 3/4" plywood to the given dimensions. Cut the plastic laminate top to roughly the same dimensions, slightly larger but no smaller. Use contact cement for plastic laminates to glue the laminate in place on the plywood following manufacturer's directions. Place the glued top face down on a flat surface and load the bottom with weights to set the laminate. When the laminate has set, rout the edges smooth and sand the cut edges of the plywood absolutely smooth by hand.

Note: You can eliminate this step by substituting ready-made laminated plywood to size.

Rip the top trim to the given dimensions, miter the corners at a 45-degree angle, round the top edge and sand smooth. The trim must make a perfect fit with the edge of the tabletop so that food and dirt won't catch between the trim and the top (see Trim). Check the fit between the two for every edge before proceeding. At this point, you should stain these strips to match the rest of the project. This way you will avoid staining the plastic laminate by finishing the strips when the table is assembled.

A water-resistant finish that is strong and durable is recommended. When the trim is dry, attach it to the top with glue and 3/4" brads spaced 6" apart.

2. Make the Apron. Cut apron pieces to the given dimensions (see Side and End Views) and then miter corners at a 45-degree angle. When the miters are cut, run the angled edges along the table of a table saw with the outside edge against the saw guard, cut 1/4"-deep slots for splines (see Apron and Leg).

Cut splines to fit from a tough wood such as maple or pieces of paneling, and apply glue to the edges of the apron and the splines. Fit the apron together, slip in the splines, then check to be sure the assembled unit is perfectly square, and clamp until set.

3. Attach the Apron. Use a doweling jig to drill 3/8" holes through the apron for countersunk 1½" roundhead wood screws. Position the apron square in the center of the tabletop and screw it down. Place the screws in the center of each of the four sides.

4. Make the Legs. Cut the legs to the given dimensions. You can build the table with square legs or with tapered legs, to give it a more graceful look. If you do taper the legs, be sure to begin the taper at the bottom of the apron, leaving the legs square inside the apron for secure attachment to the table. The legs taper from 1½" x 1½" to 1¼" x 1¼" (starting 2⅜" below their tops). Whether you taper the legs or leave them straight, you must round the edges.

5. Attach the Legs. Cut the leg braces to the given dimensions and miter the corners at a 45-degree angle. Glue and screw the braces to the inside corners of the apron, flush against the tabletop, using No. 8 x 1½"

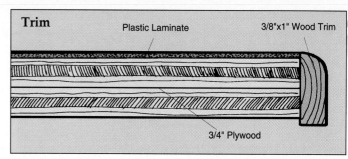

Trim — Plastic Laminate — 3/8"x1" Wood Trim — 3/4" Plywood

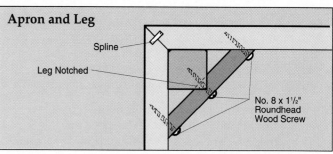

Apron and Leg — Spline — Leg Notched — No. 8 x 1½" Roundhead Wood Screw

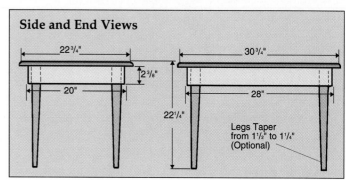

Side and End Views — 22¾" — 2⅜" — 20" — 30¾" — 28" — 22¼" — Legs Taper from 1½" to 1¼" (Optional)

roundhead wood screws. Then hold the legs in the position, mark the portion that overlaps the brace and cut a 1½"- deep notch from one corner of each leg. Apply glue to the top edges of the legs, fit the legs in place and fasten them to the apron using the roundhead wood screws.

6. Finish the Table. Sand all edges thoroughly so that they are well rounded and safe. Mask the tabletop and apply the desired decoration and finish.

How to Taper Legs

You can cut the taper on a band saw along lines you have marked. You also can cut tapers freehand, guiding the legs along a table-saw blade, or you can use a jointer. If you use a jointer, mark the straight portion of the legs (the top), and clamp a 3/8"-thick block on the joint so that when the leg is drawn against the cutting, the top of the leg will ride on the block. If you select this method, be sure to practice on scrap before trying it on the legs.

The Chairs

If you plan to make more than two chairs (either two sets of tables and chairs or four chairs, for example), cut them all at the same time to simplify the project.

1. Make the Chair Bottoms. The chair bottoms are made of 3/4" stock glued and doweled to make up the 13" x 13" dimensions (assuming that it will have to be pieced). For each bottom, lay out stock large enough to accommodate the dimensions. Use a jointer or hand plane to smooth the butted edges so they make a perfect fit; then make two parallel lines across the joints as guides for drilling the dowel holes. Use a doweling jig to drill 3/8" holes 3/4" deep where marked in the butted edges. Squeeze glue into the holes along one edge, drive in the 3/8" dowel pegs, glue the facing edge and its dowel holes and drive it onto the dowels. Clamp in a bar clamp and allow to set overnight. When the chair bottoms are dry, cut them to given dimensions, round the corners slightly and sand the edges slightly round.

2. Build the Apron. Cut the apron pieces to the given dimensions (see Side and Front Views) and sand them. Make a frame of the pieces and attach the pieces with glue and two No. 8" x 1½" brass roundhead wood screws, NOT countersunk (see Apron and Leg). These can be tightened if the legs loosen after rough use. Be sure that the apron is squared as you work.

3. Install the Apron. Position the apron in the center of the bottom of the seat, mark the position, and attach the apron with glue and 1½" flathead wood screws, countersunk into seat top. Clamp with C-clamps and allow to set overnight.

4. Cut and Install the Legs. Cut the legs to the given dimensions; then notch two adjacent corners at the tops of the legs 3/8" and 2" deep so the apron will sit over them for extra strength. Cut the corner braces to the given dimensions.

Hold one of the legs in position against the apron, measure the braces against the corners of the apron (up against the leg), and cut 45-degree miters at either end so that they will hold the legs against the apron. Install the braces and legs (see Apron and Leg) with No. 8" x 1½" roundhead wood screws.

5. Make and Install Chair Uprights and Backs.
Cut the chair backs and then the uprights to the given dimensions. Cut a 1/2" notch 2¼" deep in the front of each upright at the top. Cut the bottoms of the uprights at an 85° angle (see Side and Front Views). Bore a 5/8" hole 2" deep in the center of the bottom of each upright and in the chair bottoms, making sure to maintain the correct angle. Glue and dowel the uprights in place (see Exploded View).

Side and Front Views

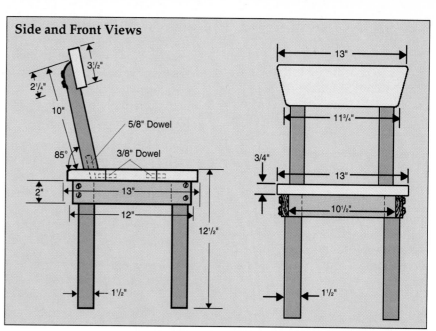

Apron and Leg

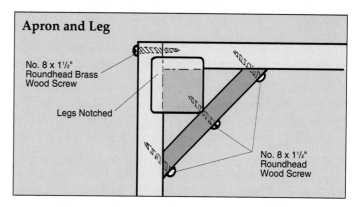

Exploded View

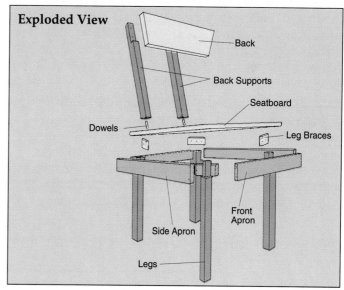

Position the chair backs in the notches in the uprights, bore screw holes, and then glue and screw the backs in place to the uprights with No. 8 x 1½" roundhead wood screws driven from the back of the uprights (see Exploded View).

6. Finish the Chairs. Sand the chairs thoroughly, then stain and finish to match the table. Add chair leg tips if desired.

Sectionalized Storage

Kitchen cabinetmakers have made it easy to coordinate the rest of a Great Room or family room in keeping with the kitchen's style. Line extensions for cabinets often are designed with multiple use and family activities in mind. Examples are open bookshelves and desk sections that meld perfectly with the cabinetry. However, inventive homeowners often have used conventional kitchen cabinet units, retrofitted for other uses, in completing a family area, basement or attic.

Kids storage and adult storage can coexist best when separated. This enables kids to completely take over the living area when adults are not also using it. When the entire family uses this space, toys and projects can be placed in storage units.

Plan a kid's storage section that is easily accessible from the family room area and away from the kitchen. That way, kids can clean up without interfering with food preparation. Plan storage close to where items are likely to be used.

Kitchen cabinets often are offered with organizers that work beautifully to store toys and other noncooking objects. Look for organizers in the form of wire baskets that extend on rollers, or are fully removable with handles. Using these units for toy and game storage can make cleaning up the family area far less of a task for both kids and parents.

If your family area connects to the kitchen and you want to match furnishings don't overlook recent designs which bring a furniture finish into the kitchen. By melding the two areas in this way, you will create a unified look.

Trophy or Model Case

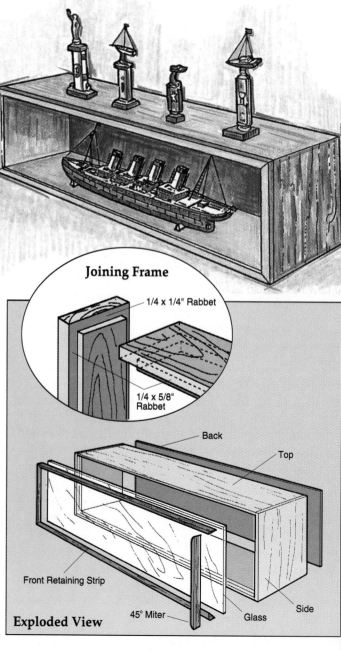

Youngsters often have models or trophies that merit special display. Any wood, finished any way, will be fine for this job.

1. Cut the Case Sides. Cut the top, bottom, and ends to the given dimensions from any 3/4" stock. Then cut or rout a 1/4" x 5/8" rabbet in the front edge of each piece and a 1/4" x 1/4" rabbet into the remaining three edges.

2. Assemble the Case. Attach the top and bottom to the sides with glue, making sure that the 5/8"-deep rabbet is at the front on all four pieces. Clamp and allow to set overnight. When dry, cut the back to the given dimensions from 1/4" hardboard or, for a stronger case, from 3/4" plywood. If you use a 3/4" back, cut a 1/4" x 1/4" rabbet around all sides so that it will fit snugly into the rabbet on the back of the case. Attach the back to the case with four 1/2" roundhead brass screws so it can be removed easily when you want to change the display. When the case is assembled, sand it all over.

3. Install the Glass Front. Cut the 1/4" x 1/4" front retaining strips to size, miter the corners at a 45-degree angle, and check to see that they fit inside the rabbeted front of the case; correct the cuts if necessary. Then stain and finish, or paint the case and front retaining strips. After the finish or paint is dry, insert the glass in the rabbeted front, glue the front retaining strips in place, and clamp with C-clamps.

Joining Frame

1/4 x 1/4" Rabbet

1/4 x 5/8" Rabbet

Tools & Materials

- ☐ (2) 3/4" x 4" x 23½" Any Stock (For case top and bottom)
- ☐ (2) 3/4" x 4" x 8" Any Stock (For case ends)
- ☐ (1) 1/4" x 7" x 23½" Hardboard or 3/4" Stock (For Back)
- ☐ (2) 1/4" x 1/4" x 23½" (For top and bottom front retaining strips)
- ☐ (2) 1/4" x 1/4" x 7" (For end front retaining strips)
- ☐ (1) 7" x 23½" Piece of Glass
- ☐ Glue   ☐ 1/2" Roundhead Brass Screws
- ☐ Paint or Stain   ☐ Table Saw or Radial Arm Saw
- ☐ Router (Optional)   ☐ Sandpaper
- ☐ Screwdriver   ☐ C-Clamps

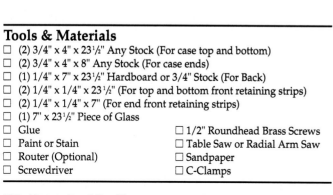

Back

Top

Front Retaining Strip

45° Miter

Glass

Side

Exploded View

Family-Oriented Flooring

Conventional kitchen flooring, sheet vinyl, vinyl tiles or tile, can be extended into a Great Room addition for a unified look. Alternatively, wood flooring can be extended from the Great Room into the kitchen, thanks to current durable wood surfaces that are impervious to kitchen staining. Monolithic flooring throughout is the best solution if the spaces are small, since they will make the entire room look larger. This is the easiest kind of floor treatment to install. Area rugs can be added to soften the effect in the Great Room area, so long as they are backed with nonskid underlayment or secured to the floor. For a painterly touch, try stenciling a design on hardwood flooring (see page 59 for directions).

A number of flooring manufacturers who make more than one kind of hard surface flooring have styled the different types to coordinate with one another. Ceramic tiles are colored to match resilient flooring and to compliment carpeting. Pale and pastel shades of woodgrain flooring are created in the same colors and designs. This calculated planning makes integrated flooring easier to create than ever before. For instance, resilient flooring can be used for the field of the kitchen floor, and surrounded in a border of ceramic tiles to match. The ceramic tiles can extend into the Great Room, which can have a field of coordinated hardwood floor. A special floor-sitting area for children can be separated off with carpeting, in tones to meld with the wood, tile and resilient floor.

Patterns such as borders unify spaces, while use of different flooring serves to set off specific areas in a Great Room. Setting off areas is particularly important with a change in level, such as a step down from the kitchen area. Even on a flat plane, consider using different types of flooring to break up a large space and define groupings and areas within a Great Room. No-nonsense tile might be ideal under a crafting area or where plants are displayed, while carpeting in a tight weave could well work best under rolling chairs at an activity table.

The considerations for Great Rooms can work as well for other areas of a house where kids are likely to congregate. Two other areas, often created especially for kids, are finished basements and attic retreats.

Install Resilient Sheet Floorcovering

Resilient sheet flooring can be installed over old flooring if it is smooth and tightly adhered to the subfloor. Concrete must be dry, level and clean. If these conditions cannot be met, install a plywood underlayer. Order flooring to arrive three days in advance to allow it time to adjust to room temperature.

Unroll sheet in a large open space to make a rough cut. Transfer the floor plan onto it with a water soluble felt-tipped pen and cut so that it is about 3" oversize all around.

You will trim excess away after the flooring has been placed. Apply adhesive according to the manufacturer's instructions. Note how much time you have before it dries.

Follow the instructions below for trimming flooring.

Install Seams. Install sections with adhesive, overlapping them as shown. Cut through the overlap to make the seam.

Trim an Outside Corner. Cut straight down the curled up flooring. Begin at the top edge and cut to where wall meets floor.

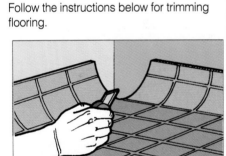

Trim an Inside Corner. Cut the excess flooring away with increasingly lower diagonal cuts on each side of the corner. Gradually the flooring will lie flat to the floor.

Trim Along Walls. Press flooring down with a long piece of 2 x 4 until it begins to develop a crease at the joint. Then position a heavy metal straightedge into the crease and cut with a utility knife, leaving a 1/8" expansion gap between edge and the wall.

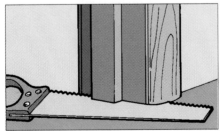

Cut Under a Doorjamb. The best way to have the flooring meet a doorjamb is to cut away a portion of the jamb so the flooring will slide under it. Trim the flooring to match the angles, overcutting about 1/2" for the edge to slip under the jamb.

Finish the Job. Clean the floor with a solvent recommended by the manufacturer. Clean up any adhesive that may have oozed up onto the surface. Then roll the flooring so that it sets firmly and flatly. Then, replace the baseboard and shoe molding.

Basement Playrooms

The major drawback for most basement spaces is a lack of light. This gold mine for kids, with ample space, can be easily converted into a desirable play room.

Windows and Lights. Use the best tricks in the business to make this room as attractive as any above-ground. Expand the impact of any existing windows by keeping window treatments to the sides of windows, not directly over them. Supplement natural daylight with plenty of artificial light to make this room bright and cheerful. Suspended ceilings are inexpensive ways of finishing off basements, and afford ample opportunity to incorporate broad spectrum fluorescent lighting which closely emulates natural light, and is healthful as well as aesthetically pleasing.

Stairway. Upgrading the stairway into a basement playroom often is the only way to make an appropriate entrance. Stairs can be redesigned so

This basement's basic black and white scheme with paint-pot accents lightens and brightens every corner.

Camouflage a Floor

Raw concrete holds stains amazingly; painted concrete is somewhat less tenacious. On painted floors, you can mask stains by splattering the surface with paint of contrasting color. Whack a loaded paint brush on a stick to create the pattern. If you try this, mask walls with newspaper and be prepared to splatter yourself.

that they have lower risers and are easier for children to climb. At the same time, strong, strategically placed stair rails help kids move along the stair safely. Bannisters and railings at both child and adult height are the safest of all.

New "carpenter's stairs," meant to be carpeted and of less than first-grade plywood, are ideal choices for basement playrooms. The carpeting itself provides traction for children as they traverse the distance, and can become a sitting and playing surface.

Walls. Paneling is an ideal material for finishing a basement, so long as it is dry. With the paneling you can set off areas with partition walls and keep a unified central room. Furnace areas, storage and workshop areas in the basements can be kept under lock and key, especially with younger children using the space.

Once the basement has been sectionalized to set off utility areas, a vast and somewhat impersonal area can remain. By using either woodgrain or patterned paneling or colorful wallcovering, a warm and

intimate feeling can be created even in a large space. Create areas by grouping furniture and play spaces with visual dividers such as area rugs that can be quickly reconfigured. One huge advantage of a basement is precisely its size—on a rainy day it can become anything from a miniature Indianapolis speedway to a cowboy town.

Carpet Tile

Carpet tile is easy to use, even for the beginner. Pieces are laid in the same way as resilient tile is laid (see instructions next page).

Applying Self-Stick Tiles. Peel the protective backing from the self-sticking, or foam-backed tiles. Align the tile exactly before placing it. Firmly press the entire surface of the tile to seat it securely.

Using Carpet Adhesive. Use a trowel to spread adhesive over the floor. Follow the manufacturer's instructions carefully. Position the tiles exactly and press them down firmly. Do not slide them around.

Install Resilient Tile

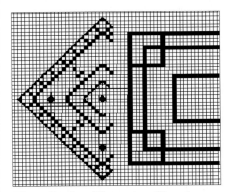

Plot a Design. When using different colors, plot out the design on graph paper using one square for each tile.

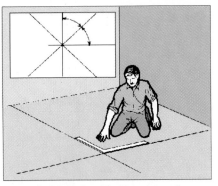

Mark Guidelines. Measure the walls to find their midpoints and stretch strings or chalk lines between them; add diagonals as described for diagonal designs.

Adjust Guidelines or Pattern. Lay out tiles along two of the guidelines and check the fit at the walls; adjust the lines as necessary.

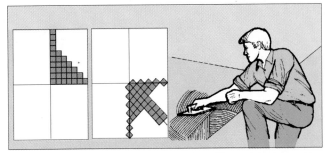

Set Tiles in Adhesive. Apply adhesive with a notched trowel in one quadrant, leaving the guidelines visible. Set the first tile at the intersection of the guidelines, dropping—not sliding—it into place.

Trim Border. Set two tiles atop the one closest to the wall. Slide the top tile against the wall, and mark the one beneath. Score the marked tile with a utility knife; break it along the line.

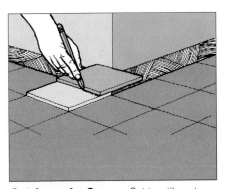

Cut Around a Corner. Set two tiles atop the tile closest to one side of the corner to be cut out, mark that dimension, then shift the two tiles to the other side of the corner to mark the other dimension.

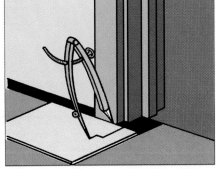

Cut Around Molding. Run one compass leg along the molding. The other draws the outline on the tile.

Cut Around an Obstruction. Make a paper pattern to fit around obstructions. Trace onto the tile.

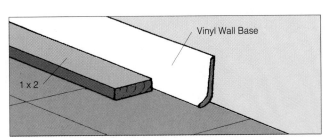

Install Base Molding. A vinyl wall base is a practical option. Use a glass jar or a steel hand roller to roll the base. Then, use a 1x2 to press the bottom of the base firmly against the wall.

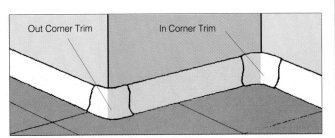

Install Corner Molding. Preformed inside and outside corners provide a neater look for a continuous base line.

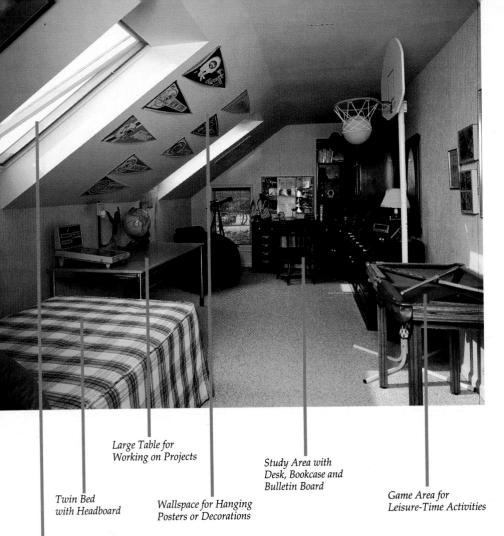

Attic Retreats

What child wouldn't love to have a tree house right in his own home! Attic play spaces have that feeling. Odd angles of sloping ceilings and sidewalls are great decorative advantages here. Soft carpeting throughout an attic serves to unify the angles and will temper noises that might be transmitted to the rooms below. Long-lasting foam-back carpeting is a sturdy choice, and is installed with adhesive. Look for one with a stain-resistant surface, making cleanup easy.

Conventional knee walls in attic renovations are 5' high, with the width of the space determined by where this 5' height occurs. However, kids will be just as happy with walls of as little as 2' to 3' in height, affording much greater playing surface on the floor. Add storage benches to the knee walls to make optimum use of the space.

Windows. Advances in skylights will enable you to find just the right one for any attic conversion. Simple stationary bump-out skylights will open up an attic space enormously. Moveable skylights can include built-in shades, automated opening and closing, tinted glass and other features. Plan where you will be

Large Table for Working on Projects

Study Area with Desk, Bookcase and Bulletin Board

Twin Bed with Headboard

Wallspace for Hanging Posters or Decorations

Game Area for Leisure-Time Activities

Skylight Windows for an Open Look and for Ventilation

Hip walls lend themselves to built-in counters and storage, exemplified in this room.

Install Foam-Back Carpeting

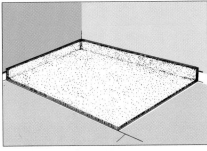

Align Carpet Sections. Spread out the carpeting like a large blanket, aligning the edges with prestruck chalk lines.

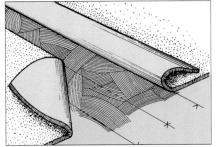

Spread Adhesive at Seams. Spread the adhesive on the floor and set the carpeting against the chalk line guides.

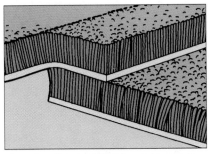

Overlap Carpet Sections. To match seams, overlap one section of carpeting with the other about 1/4".

Apply Seaming Fluid. Apply seaming fluid along the backing of one edge of the carpeting. Work seam together so the edges match perfectly.

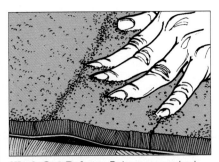

Work Out Bulges. Bulges are worked out at the seams with your fingers. Work from seam outward, across carpeting, eliminating bubbles.

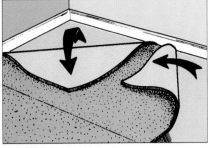

Fold Back Carpet. When seams are set, fold carpeting back at the corners.

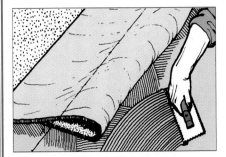

Spread Adhesive on Floor. Use a notched spreader to apply adhesive to the floor. Then fold the carpeting back into the adhesive.

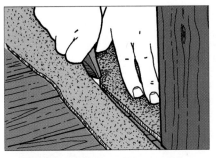

Trim Excess Carpet. Trim carpeting with utility knife. Go over carpeting with hammer and wooden block.

A pretty dormer window allows the sunshine to come through while creating an open ceiling line.

placing the furniture and other elements in conjunction to the skylight. You also will want to consider the path and position of the sun, availability of shade on hot summer days, and potential views from any skylight.

Dormer windows are traditional additions that add both space and light to an attic renovation. Double- and triple- dormer windows can create new useable space.

Stairs. Do not overlook the stairways that tie an attic playroom to the rest of the house. Be sure that railings and other safety measures are built-in or added. Lighting on this stairway must be easily accessed from either the floor below or within the attic itself. Make sure that the stairs are physically set off from the rest of the attic play space, so that children who are roughhousing will not tumble downstairs.

Insulation. When considering an attic for a play space, remember that overhead room needs to be allocated to insulation and ventilation.

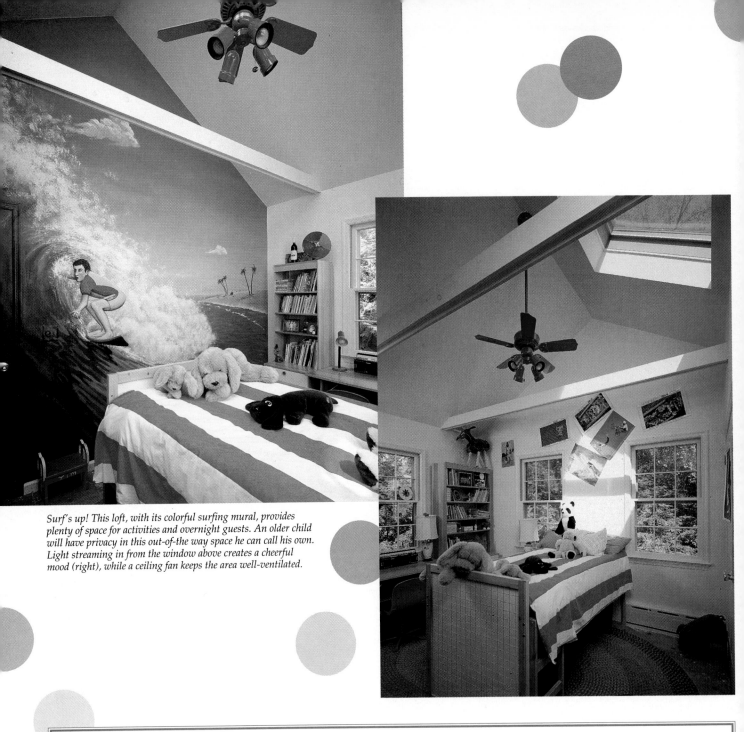

Surf's up! This loft, with its colorful surfing mural, provides plenty of space for activities and overnight guests. An older child will have privacy in this out-of-the-way space he can call his own. Light streaming in from the window above creates a cheerful mood (right), while a ceiling fan keeps the area well-ventilated.

Attic Insulation

The main reason for insulating is to lower the cost of heating and cooling. The more insulation your home has, the less heat flow to and from the outside will occur. A home that is sealed from the weather is comfortable at 65 to 68°F during the winter, while a home that is not properly insulated requires a temperature at least three degrees higher to achieve a similar level of comfort. You will need to insulate under the roof when you refinish an attic, allowing sufficient space for ventilation. By insulating the attic, you increase the value of your home, while conserving natural resources. Insulation in the attic floor reduces noise levels in the home.

Batts and Blankets. Often used by do-it-yourselfers, batts and blankets are made from either rock wool or, more commonly fiberglass. Blankets are continuous rolls that are hand-cut to fit the application. Batts come in precut 4' and 8' lengths; and both of them come in 16" and 24" widths and are available with a foil or paper facing as a vapor barrier. Batts and blankets cannot be used in existing finished walls without first removing the finish material on one side.

R-Values. The R-value needed for your attic depends on the type of insulation to be used and the climate in which you live. The U.S. Department of Energy recommends R-11 for all exterior walls located in the continental U.S. However, you may wish to use a higher R-value. Call your local building department for the recommended R-values in your area.

Where It Should Go. Place sufficient insulation between the studs in the walls and between the rafters or ceiling joists, whichever is in the middle of heated and unheated space or where noise reduction is desired.

Mud Rooms & Other Entrances

Make a special place for the ins and outs of life. Preparing children for the outdoors and setting them up to dress themselves comes easiest when you've set aside a special area for just this purpose. If you don't have a specific mud room (so named because it is a room that's designed for accommodating tracking from outside before entering the rest of the house), carve such an area out of space just inside an outer doorway. Ideally, this entrance is in the garage or off of the kitchen.

Flooring. In the mud room, the flooring should be easy to care for and water-resistant. Walls also should resist staining and water damage. You can set up a row of hooks (low enough for a child to use) to hold favorite coats, hats and scarves. Provide additional storage for the alternate gloves, mittens, hats and scarves children may want to wear.

Organization and Accessories. Separate drawers for more than one child can eliminate confusion. Open shelving with attractive baskets to hold accessories will allow children to make their own clothing decisions. A hamper, for depositing soiled clothes right at the door, handles the problem instantly. The dirty laundry is just waiting for your next washing.

You also may want pegs or hooks for towels to use during inclement weather. Kids can be dried off right at the door where they need it the most.

Shoes and boots, dirtied from outside, also need a place to be located. Stacked waterproof shelves can consolidate footwear in one small area, or you can set aside a part of the floor for this purpose.

An umbrella stand and specific area for any toys that are brought inside, balls to butterfly nets, need to be factored in. A table for unloading school books and lunch boxes will be used on a daily basis. If you have two children, you may want to double the size, or provide each child with his own shelf.

Children as well as adults need a mirror for last-minute checking of their outfits and grooming. Be sure that any mirror is placed at an accommodating height.

Pet Needs. Pet paraphernalia also needs to be stored near a door, and a mud room is a logical place to put it.

Seating. For putting on boots and taking them off, seating is a necessary ingredient for any mud room. Whether children use the seating to dress themselves or you seat the child so you can put on her shoes and boots, you'll find it's really helpful.

Any kind of seating is fine for a mud room, so long as it is properly sized for the child. However, if the child is not old enough to dress herself, you may need the seat to be a more appropriate size for you. These pieces can be whimsical if the mud room is separated from the rest of the house. Or, if the area is part of a larger room, you will want to select seating that echoes the design found in the rest of the home.

Style. Mostly, casual styles are in order in a mud room, reflecting the utilitarian nature of the area itself. However, you can be as fanciful as you want in decorating. Shaker storage benches, Early American-style settles, upholstered Victorian slipper chairs, or contemporary built-in storage bench units are all possibilities.

Keep in mind, the entrance of the home creates a first impression. An enchanting mud room entrance welcomes all with the warmth and good feelings that go along with a loving and a loved childhood.

Along with an easy-to-clean floor, and a table and chairs for removing boots and putting down packages, this long entrance hall and mud room features a detailed mural of the Nantucket harbor view.

Appendix A

Floor Plans

A solid plan is your best strategy for avoiding any decorating disasters. No matter how large the area of a child's room (and many are pretty small), efficient use of space is your greatest resource. Like the slight variation on an old carpenter's saying "measure twice and cut once," your best bet is to measure twice and purchase furniture that fits the space.

Start with 1/4" graph paper, or photocopy the sample on the next page, with the scale, one square=one foot. Draw the outline of the room you are planning, including architectural details such as windows and doors (don't forget to note which way the door swings), electrical outlets, heat and air conditioning outlets, riser pipes, niches, etc. Make a photocopy or tracing of the furniture templates shown on page 120-121, select those that closest represent the furniture you plan to use, and arrange them on paper. Measurements for these pieces are given in length, width and height respectively.

In planning the arrangement, keep the following in mind:

Clearances. There should be enough space around furniture to use it comfortably. For instance, leave space for a chair to be pulled out at a desk; and allow space to make a bed. Also, enough space should be provided for clearance of baseboard heating or heat vents and air conditioning. Clearances will vary depending upon the size of the furniture. One advantage of small-scale furniture is that it fits into smaller spaces.

Some general clearance guidelines:

■ Beds: 22" clearance needed for making

■ Closets: 3' needed for dressing and sorting

■ Dressers: 40" needed for opening drawers

■ TV Viewing: At least 1½ times screen diagonal for small screen and 2½ times screen diagonal for home theaters.

■ Base Heaters: 6" to 1', (use manufacturer's instructions for other heating and cooling clearances)

Traffic Patterns. Once you have a preliminary floor plan, estimate the traffic patterns that will take place in the room. Make them as convenient as possible for you and your children. For example, in a nursery, you may want the changing table closest to the door and the crib farther into the room. Then you'll be able to resupply the changing table without disturbing a sleeping baby.

Traffic patterns are especially important in shared rooms. Allow clearances for one child to pass another without disruption when someone is seated at a desk or play area. Storage areas placed where kids play will be used more than those inconveniently located.

Adaptability. If you're planning to stay in the same house, note how the furniture and its arrangement can be adapted to future needs. Obviously, a youth or twin bed will take up more space than a crib, so make sure dressers, armoires, and other furniture will still fit. Floor plans that detail future needs as well as present needs can help guide you in furniture selections. See the sample floor plans below.

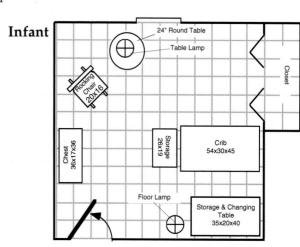

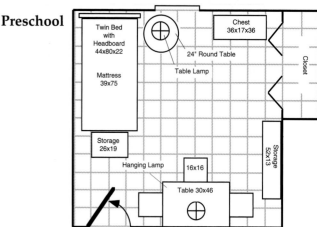

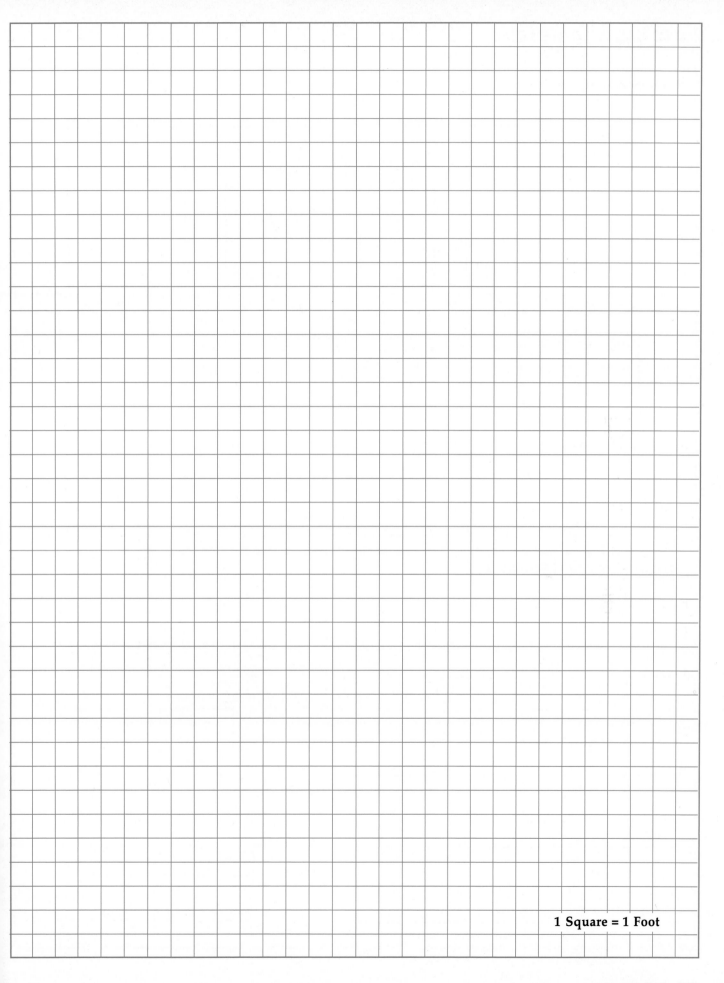

1 Square = 1 Foot

Furniture Templates

Beds and Sofa Beds

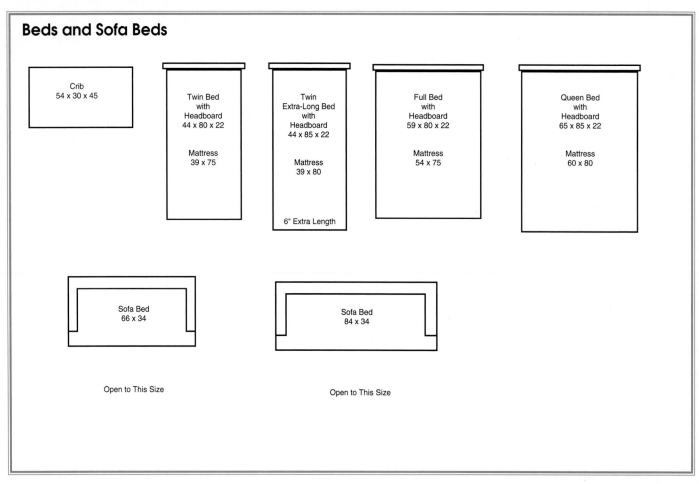

Crib
54 x 30 x 45

Twin Bed
with
Headboard
44 x 80 x 22

Mattress
39 x 75

Twin
Extra-Long Bed
with
Headboard
44 x 85 x 22

Mattress
39 x 80

6" Extra Length

Full Bed
with
Headboard
59 x 80 x 22

Mattress
54 x 75

Queen Bed
with
Headboard
65 x 85 x 22

Mattress
60 x 80

Sofa Bed
66 x 34

Sofa Bed
84 x 34

Open to This Size

Open to This Size

Storage Units and Bookcases

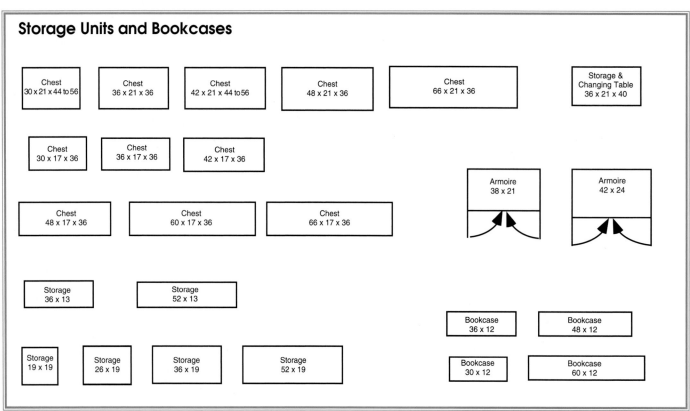

Chest
30 x 21 x 44 to 56

Chest
36 x 21 x 36

Chest
42 x 21 x 44 to 56

Chest
48 x 21 x 36

Chest
66 x 21 x 36

Storage &
Changing Table
36 x 21 x 40

Chest
30 x 17 x 36

Chest
36 x 17 x 36

Chest
42 x 17 x 36

Chest
48 x 17 x 36

Chest
60 x 17 x 36

Chest
66 x 17 x 36

Armoire
38 x 21

Armoire
42 x 24

Storage
36 x 13

Storage
52 x 13

Bookcase
36 x 12

Bookcase
48 x 12

Storage
19 x 19

Storage
26 x 19

Storage
36 x 19

Storage
52 x 19

Bookcase
30 x 12

Bookcase
60 x 12

Sofas and Chairs

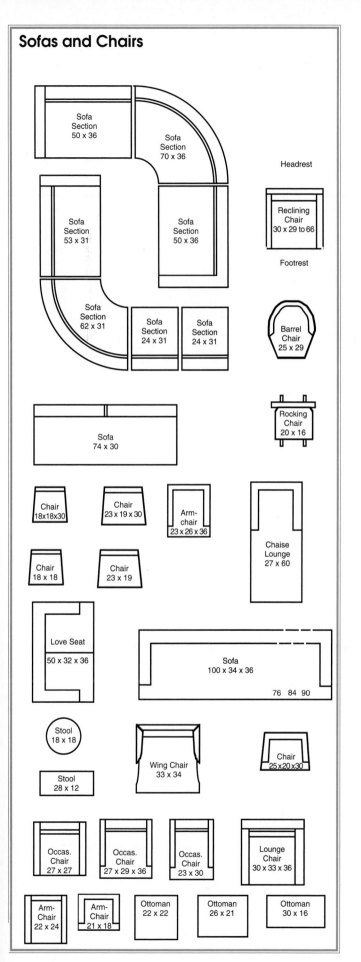

Sofa Section 50 x 36

Sofa Section 70 x 36

Sofa Section 53 x 31

Sofa Section 50 x 36

Sofa Section 62 x 31

Sofa Section 24 x 31

Sofa Section 24 x 31

Headrest

Reclining Chair 30 x 29 to 66

Footrest

Barrel Chair 25 x 29

Rocking Chair 20 x 16

Sofa 74 x 30

Chair 18x18x30

Chair 23 x 19 x 30

Arm-chair 23 x 26 x 36

Chaise Lounge 27 x 60

Chair 18 x 18

Chair 23 x 19

Love Seat 50 x 32 x 36

Sofa 100 x 34 x 36

76 84 90

Stool 18 x 18

Wing Chair 33 x 34

Chair 25 x 20 x30

Stool 28 x 12

Occas. Chair 27 x 27

Occas. Chair 27 x 29 x 36

Occas. Chair 23 x 30

Lounge Chair 30 x 33 x 36

Arm-Chair 22 x 24

Arm-Chair 21 x 18

Ottoman 22 x 22

Ottoman 26 x 21

Ottoman 30 x 16

Tables and Desks

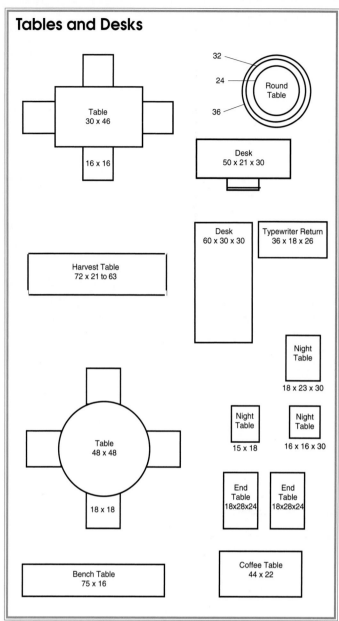

Table 30 x 46

16 x 16

32
24
36
Round Table

Desk 50 x 21 x 30

Desk 60 x 30 x 30

Typewriter Return 36 x 18 x 26

Harvest Table 72 x 21 to 63

Night Table 18 x 23 x 30

Night Table 15 x 18

Night Table 16 x 16 x 30

Table 48 x 48

18 x 18

End Table 18x28x24

End Table 18x28x24

Coffee Table 44 x 22

Bench Table 75 x 16

Miscellaneous Furniture

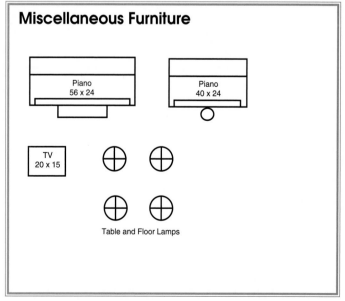

Piano 56 x 24

Piano 40 x 24

TV 20 x 15

Table and Floor Lamps

Appendix B

Budget & Plan Worksheet

What follows are preliminary listings of the various items that must be coordinated to create children's rooms. Use the items below, or add selections that reflect your own personal needs and tastes.

Armed with your budget plan and the layout of a child's room, you are ready to outfit any kid's space with ease and keep within a budget. You also can use it as a basis for future additions as your children grow.

Sample Worksheet:

Item	Description Style/Color	Use Existing	Restore Existing	Immediate Purchase	Future Purchase	Estimated Cost
☐ Crib	Annie's old pine crib	✔				.00
☐ Rocker (Adult)	Grandma's pine ladderback		✔			50.00
☐ Changing Table	Pine (to match crib)			✔		105.00
☐ Rug	Large rag rug (pastels)			✔		150.00
☐ Game or Activity Table	Table for cards, puzzles				✔	150.00
TOTAL COST:						**$ 455.00**

Item	Description Style/Color	Use Existing	Restore Existing	Immediate Purchase	Future Purchase	Estimated Cost
Bedroom Furniture:						
☐ Crib						
☐ Bed						
☐ Bunk Beds						
☐ Changing Table						
☐ Chest						
☐ Dresser						
☐ Armoire						
☐ Arm Chair (Adult)						
☐ Rocker (Adult)						
☐ Play Table						
☐ Play Chairs						
☐ Desk						
☐ Desk Chair						
☐ Vanity						
☐ Bookcase(s)						
☐ Side Table						
☐						
☐						
Playroom Furniture:						
☐ Sofa(s)						
☐ Sofa Bed						
☐ Lounge Chair(s)						
☐ Motion Chair(s)						
☐ Modular Sofa						
☐ End Tables						
☐ Coffee Tables						
☐ Game or Activity Table						
☐ Storage Cabinets						

Item	Description Style/Color	Use Existing	Restore Existing	Immediate Purchase	Future Purchase	Estimated Cost
☐ Wall System(s)						
☐ Exercise Equipment						
☐						
☐						
Floors:						
☐ Carpeting						
☐ Rug						
☐ Wood Flooring						
☐ Resilient Flooring						
☐						
☐						
Wall Treatments:						
☐ Paint						
☐ Wallcovering						
☐ Fabric						
☐ Paneling						
☐						
☐						
Window Treatments:						
☐ Curtains						
☐ Shades						
☐ Blinds						
☐ Draperies						
☐						
☐						
Lighting/Electrical:						
☐ Track Lights						
☐ Lamps						
☐ Night-Light						
☐ Fixtures						
☐ Intercom						
☐ Fire Alarm						
☐ Television						
☐ Sound Equipment						
☐ Computer & Desk						
☐						
☐						
Accessories:						
☐ Bedspread						
☐ Sheets						
☐ Pillows						
☐ Mirrors						
☐ Wall Art						
☐ Bulletin Board						
☐						
☐						
TOTAL COST:						

Glossary

Anthropometry. The science and technique of human measurements, especially anatomical and physiological features.

Ballast, electric. The part of a fluorescent lamp that stabilizes current which is then delivered to the bulb.

Bar clamp. A variation of the C-clamp, consisting of a steel bar with a fixed jaw at one end and a sliding or adjustable swivel jaw at the other.

Baseboard and baseboard shoe. A piece of trim either plain or milled, installed around a room at the base of walls to conceal the joints of walls and adjoining floor covering. Shoe is a narrow piece of trim, usually a quarter round, attached to baseboard to hide gaps.

Building code. The rules and regulations governing the acceptable specifications and building types allowed in a city or town. Local building permits are almost always required for new construction or major renovation.

Broadknife. A wide putty knife, used in trimming wallcoverings.

C-clamp. A steel framed clamp (shaped like a "C") threaded at one end to receive an operating screw with a swivel head that is adjusted with a sliding pin handle.

Chair rail. A horizontal strip of molding mounted at the proper height to prevent the top of a chair back from touching a wall surface.

Counterbore. Use of a counterbore drill bit to bore a hole at the end of a pilot hole in order to accommodate a wood plug or other covering to hide a screw head.

Countersink. Similar to counterboring, drilling deep enough so that a flathead screw sits slightly below the surface face when driven in.

Dado. A square "U" shaped groove cut into the face of a board to receive and support the end of another board.

Decoupage. An art form popular since the 18th century; assorted materials are arranged in interesting new relationships, cut, pasted down and sealed.

Dovetail. In cabinetry, a type of joint used to join the front and sides of a drawer, with wedge-shaped projections on one piece of wood interlocking with alternating grooves in the other piece to produce a tight, secure joint.

Dust panel or board. A thin wood separator between drawers to keep out dust that may enter through open spaces.

Dowel. A wood pin used to join two pieces of wood. It fits into holes drilled in each piece, creating a dowel joint.

Footcandle. A unit of measurement for light, based on the amount produced by a standard candle at a one foot distance.

Ergonomics. The study of man's behavior in relation to his work.

Grain. The growth pattern in a tree. Grain looks different in different trees and as a result of different sawing techniques. Usually has a decided direction.

Ground fault circuit interrupter (GFCI). A special circuit breaker that reacts to an improper electrical circuit condition such as a sudden overcurrent demand (short circuit) in a fraction of a second, demanded by code in many kitchen and bath installations.

Hardwood. Wood cut from deciduous (leaf-bearing) trees. Used as solids and as face veneer for some plywood.

Jig saw. Also known as a saber saw, the jig saw is a power tool designed especially to cut wood curves and internal cutouts.

Jointer. A long plane used to smooth the lumber surface prior to gluing or cutting, and to make common joints, such as rabbets, bevels and tongues.

Joint. A junction of two pieces of wood or veneer.

Joist. A floor or ceiling support member that runs between opposite walls of a room and rests on the top plates of bearing walls.

Kerf. The space created by a saw blade as it cuts through wood. All cuts should be made on the outside, or waste side, of lines marked for cutting so that the inside edge of the kerf just touches the mark.

Knee wall. A wall built under a sloping roof, does not reach apex of the ceiling.

Lathe. A machine designed to hold wood in place while spinning it, frequently used in making chair legs.

Miter. To cut a beveled edge on a piece of lumber for the purpose of making a miter joint. A miter joint usually is the mating of two 45-degree angled ends to make a 90-degree corner.

Molding. Various types of wood used for decorative or practical trim.

Paneling. Planks or sheets used as a finished wall or ceiling surface, often with a wood, or simulated wood finish.

Pilot holes. Holes drilled in stock to make it easier to drive a screw through the stock. Pilot holes are slightly narrower than the diameter of the screw to be used.

Plywood. Thin sheets of veneer are sandwiched in crisscross layers of alternating grains to create dimensional stability, and laminated together. Used in furniture, often with hardwood face veneers on both sides.

Plastic laminate. A hard-surface, thin material used for the finished surfaces of countertops, cabinets and furniture.

Particleboard. A material composed of wood particles and a bonding agent to create a monolithic surface as a substrate for laminate or veneer, sometimes used without a surfacing material in less expensive furniture.

"R" value. A measure of the resistance to heat passing through a product such as windows walls or insulation. Higher "R" values indicate better insulating qualities.

Rabbet. A square "L" shaped groove cut into the edge of a board to receive the edge of another board to form a corner joint.

Radial arm saw. A stationary power saw used primarily to cut wood. Wood is fixed in place and the saw pulled over it. Accessories enable its use for sanding, shaping and cutting grooves.

Rails and styles. The horizontal members of a panel or piece of furniture. Styles are the vertical strips.

Resilient flooring. Thin, flexible floor covering in vinyl tile or sheet or rubber.

Router. A portable, versatile cutting machine which is fitted with various cutting bits and used for edging, carving, incising, piercing and cutting dadoes, grooves and many common joints.

Shaper. A power machine used for forming edges on wood.

Skylight. A window designed for use in a roof, either fixed or adjustable.

Starter hole. A small hole drilled inside the outline of a section to be cut out, so that the blade of a saw can be inserted through the hole to finish the cutting.

Table saw. A stationary power saw used mainly for crosscutting, ripping, cutting wood to size and making dadoes and grooves. Work is passed over the spinning circular blade.

Traffic pattern. The path of movement into, through and out of an area or room.

Underlayment. Sheet material placed over a subfloor or old floor covering to provide a smooth, even surface.

Veneer tape. A length of narrow veneer wood glued to an edge of plywood.

Wainscot. Paneling that covers the lower part of a wall usually 30" to 42" high, often capped by a chair rail.

Wood filler. Materials designed to fill in holes or grain lines to provide a smooth surface for finish materials.

Acknowledgements

The following companies and associations are extremely useful resources for the products and information included in this book. We are grateful for their contributions.

Aiphone Corp.
1700 130th Ave. N. E.
Bellevue, WA 98005
(206) 455-0510

Andersen Windows
Anderson Corp.
Bayport, MN 55003
(612) 439-5150

Armstrong World Industries
P. O. Box 3001
Lancaster, PA 17604
(800) 233-3823

Laura Ashley Home
714 Madison Ave.
New York, NY 10021
(212) 735-5039

Broyhill Furniture Industries, Inc.
One Broyhill Park
Lenoir, NC 28633
(704) 847-7757

Bruce Hardwood Floors
P. O. Box 660100
Dallas, TX 75266-0100
(214) 931-3100

Build-it-Square
R. C. Company
P. O. Box 595
Industrial Park
Rush City, MN 55069
(800) 356-7699

Child Craft Industries, Inc.
501 East Market St.
P. O. Box 444
Salem, IN 47167-0444
(812) 883-3111

CHF Industries, Inc.
One Park Ave.
New York, NY 10016
(212) 951-7800

Closet Maid Clairson International
720 S. W. 17th St.
Ocala, FL 32674
(904) 351-6100

Essex Wallcovering
GenCorp Polymer Products
3 University Plaza, Suite 200
Hackensack, NJ 07001
(201) 489-0100

Environmental Graphics
5295 Minnetonka Blvd.
Minnetonka, MN 55345
(612) 938-1300

Fisher-Price
636 Girard Ave.
East Aurora, NY 14052
(716) 687-3000

Funtech, Inc.
Home Safety Division
388 N. Ellicott Creek Rd.
Amherst, NY 14228
(800) 887-1250

Georgia Pacific Corp.
133 Peachtree St. N. E.
Atlanta, GA 30303
(800) 447-2882

Gerry Baby Products Co.
12520 Grant Dr.
Denver, CO 80241
(800) 626-2996

Honeywell, Inc.
Home and Building Control
1985 Douglas Drive N.
Golden Valley, MN 55422
(612) 542-3339

Hunter Douglas
2 Park Way & Route 17 S.
Upper Saddle River, NJ 07458
(800) 32-STYLE

Little Kids, Inc.
2757 Pawtucket Ave.
East Providence, RI 02914
(401) 435-4120

Marimekko
Div. of Internatinal Wallcoverings
151 East Drive
Brampton,Ontario L6TlB5
Canada
(416) 791-1547

Minwax
15 Mercedes Dr.
Montvale, NJ 07645
(201) 391-0253

Lynn Peterson
Motif Designs
20 Jones St.
New Rochelle, NY 10801
(914) 633-1170

Osram Sylvania Inc.
100 Endicott St.
Danvers, MA 01923
(508) 777-1900

Panasonic
One Panasonic Way
Secaucus, NJ 07094
(201) 348-7000

Perfectly Safe Catalogue
7245 Whipple Ave. N. W.
North Canton, OH 44720
(800) 837-KIDS

Pickardt & Siebert (USA) Inc.
P. S. USA Wallcoverings
700 Prince George's Boulevard
Upper Marlboro, MD 20772
(301) 249-7900

Priss Prints, Inc.
3960 Broadway Blvd., Suite 105
Garland, TX 75043
(800) 543-4971

Railnet Corp.
P. O. Box 7652
Boise, ID 83707
(208) 377-2844

Rohl Corp., KWC Faucets
1559 Sunland Lane
Costa Mesa, CA 92626
(714) 557-1933

Rutt Custom Kitchens
Route 23
Goodville, PA 17528
(215) 445-6751

Sanitas Wallcovering
GenCorp Polymer Products
3 University Plaza, Suite 200
Hackensack, NJ 07001
(201) 489-0100

Sauder Woodworking Co.
502 Middle St.
Archbold, OH 43502
(800) 523-3987

Step 2 Corp.
2200 Highland Rd.
P. O. Box 444
Twinsburg, OH 44087
(216) 425-1404

Sunworthy Wallcoverings
Borden Consumer Response
180 E. Broad St.
Columbus, OH 43215
(614) 225-4511

Toddler Bobbler Products Inc.
1035 Tory Ave., # 16
Pickering, Ontario LIW3N9
Canada
(416) 619-1600

U-Bild
P. O. Box 2383
Van Nuys, CA 91409
(818) 785-6368

Village Wallcoverings
79 Madison Ave.
New York, NY 10016
(800) 552-9255

Wall-Tex Wallcoverings
Borden Consumer Response 1
180 East Broad St.
Columbus, OH 43215
(614) 225-4511

These associations are of particular help.

American Academy of Pediatrics
141 Northwest Point Blvd.
P. O. Box 927
Elk Grove Village, IL 60009-0927
(708) 228-5005

American Institute of Architects
1735 New York Ave. N. W.
Washington, DC 20006
(202) 626-7300

American Furniture
Manufacturer's Association
P. O. Box HP - 7
High Point, NC 27261
(919) 884-5000

American Society of Interior
Designers
608 Massachusetts Ave. N. E.
Washington, DC 20002-6006
(202) 546-3480

American Society for Testing and
Materials (ASTM)
1916 Race St.
Philadelphia, PA 19103
(215) 299-5400

Better Sleep Council
333 Commerce St.
Alexandria, VA 22304
(703) 683-8371

U.S. Consumer Product Safety
Commission
Office of Public Information and
Public Affairs
Washington, DC 20207
800) 638-CPSC

Custom Electronic Design &
Installation Association
10400 Roberts Rd.
Palos Hills, IL 60465
(800) CEDIA-30

Juvenile Products Manufacturers
Association, Inc.
2 Greentree Centre, Suite 225
P. O. Box 955
Marlton, NJ 08053
(609) 985-2878

National Kitchen & Bath
Association
687 Willow Grove St.
Hackettstown, NJ 07840
(800) FOR-NKBA

National Safety Council
444 N. Michigan Ave.
Chicago, IL 60611-3991
(312) 527-4800

Safe Kids Campaign
111 Michigan Ave. N. W.
Washington, DC 20010-2970
(202) 939-4993

Toy Manufacturer's of America
200 Fifth Ave.
New York, NY 10010
(212) 675-1141

Upholstered Furniture
Action Council
Box 2436
High Point, NC 27261
(919) 885-5065

The Wool Bureau, Inc.
360 Lexington Ave.
New York, NY 10017
(212) 986-6222

Our special thanks also to the following agencies.

Brooks Rodgers, New York, NY

Burton Luch Public Relations, Inc.
New York, NY

Chapman Jones, New York, NY

David S. Roher, Inc., New York, NY

Doc-Anderson Agency
Louisville, KY

Drucilla Handi Co., New York, NY

Gavin Anderson Co.
New York, NY

Gaskins Creative Communications
Glendale, CA

Gilbert, Whitney, Johns
Whippany, NJ

Harold Imber, Mt. Kisco, NY

Liz King Associates, Mahwah, NJ

Photography

Aiphone Corp., 16 (right)

Armstrong World Industries, 53 (top), 54

Laura Ashley, 8, 53 (bottom), 71

Broyhill, 18

Bruce Hardwood Floors, 57 (bottom)

Built-It-Square, 36 (top)

CEDIA, 106 (bottom)

Childcraft, 9 (bottom), 25

CHF Industries, 73 (top)

Closet Maid, 37 (top right)

Essex Wallcovering, 65 (top right), 106 (top)

Everette Short Studios, 21 (bottom), 38 (top)

Fisher Price, 36 (bottom)

Funtech Home Safety, 14 (top right)

Gerry Baby Products, Inc., 14 (middle), 15, 75, 101 (bottom)

Thomas Hahn, 93

Ted Harden, 112

Nancy Hill, 19 (top and bottom), 114 (bottom), 117

Lynn Hollyn, 12 (top), 24 (top), 37 (top left), 38 (bottom), 51 (top), 61, 85 (bottom)

Honeywell, 82 (top)

Hunter Douglas, 72 (middle and bottom), 82 (bottom)

Marimekko, 21 (top left)

Norman McGrath, 12 (middle), 21 (top right), 23, 70, 100, 101 (top), 104 (top and bottom), 114 (top), 116 (top and bottom)

Melabee M. Miller, 4, 22, 64, 73 (middle), 97 (top)

Minwax, 45

Motif Designs, Inc., back cover (middle and bottom), 3 (middle and bottom), 10, 83, 98

Panasonic, 77

Parsekian/Gensheimer Photography, 16, 85, 91

Perfectly Safe, 93

Priss Prints, 9 (top), 55

PS Wallcoverings, back cover (top), 3 (top), 6, 7

Phillip H. Ennis Photography 59, 60

Railnet, 14 (bottom)

Rohl Corp., KWC Faucets, 103

Bill Rothschild, 12 (bottom), 53 (middle), 56, 62, 72 (top), 73 (top and bottom), 74, 84, 85 (top), 90, 96 (top and bottom), 97 (bottom)

Rutt, 20

Safe Kids, 102

Sauder, 24 (bottom)

Step 2 Corp., 92

Sunworthy Wallcoverings, 48, 51 (bottom), 68

Toddler Bobber, 93

Village Wallcoverings, 50, 52, 115

Wall-Tex Wallcovering, 65 (top left)

Designers

Betty Barbatsuly, ASID, Garden City, NY, 72 (top)

Harry Williams (Builder), Robbinsville, NJ, 104 (top and bottom)

Judith Cohen Interior Design, Scarsdale, NY, 19, 114 (bottom)

Joyce Dixon, Upper Saddle River, NJ, 73 (middle)

Rene Hennessy, RBH Interiors, Freehold, NY, 22

Herborg Interiors, Sinopia Decorative Painting, West Orange, NJ, 60

Lynn Hollyn Designs, New York, NY, 12 (top), 24 (top), 37 (top left), 38 (bottom), 51 (top), 61, 85 (bottom)

Karyne Johnson of Panache Interiors, Darien, CT, 19

Allyn Kandel, Roslyn, NY, 56

JoAnne Kuchner for Wilton Hills, Wilton Hills, NJ, 23

Katie Lee (Muralist), South Salem, NY, 117

Jeanne Leonard, W. Hampton Beach, NY, 73 (top)

Joan Lerner, ASID, N. Caldwell, NY, 16 (left), 85 (bottom), 91

Logan/Kuhl, Garden City, NY, 12 (middle)

Virginia Smith Interior Design, Ho-Ho-Kus, NJ, 4

Sandy Rosen, Menchen, NJ, 97 (top)

Timi Bates, Allied ASID & IDS, Timi II Interiors, Huntington, NY, 63

Index

Conversion Charts

Dimensional Lumber

Nominal Size (You order) Inches	Actual Size (You get) Inches	Nominal Size (You order) Inches	Actual Size (You get) Inches
1 x 1	3/4 x 3/4	2 x 2	$1^3/_4$ x $1^3/_4$
1 x 2	3/4 x $1^1/_2$	2 x 3	$1^1/_2$ x $2^1/_2$
1 x 3	3/4 x $2^1/_2$	2 x 4	$1^1/_2$ x $3^1/_2$
1 x 4	3/4 x $3^1/_2$	2 x 6	$1^1/_2$ x $5^1/_2$
1 x 6	3/4 x $5^1/_2$	2 x 8	$1^1/_2$ x $7^1/_4$
1 x 8	3/4 x $7^1/_4$	2 x 10	$1^1/_2$ x $9^1/_4$
1 x 10	3/4 x $9^1/_4$	2 x 12	$1^1/_2$ x $11^1/_4$
1 x 12	3/4 x $11^1/_4$		

Metric Length

Lengths in Meters	Equivalent Feet and Inches	Lengths in Meters	Equivalent Feet and Inches
1.8m	5' $10^7/_8$"	5.1m	16' $8^3/_4$"
2.1m	6' $10^5/_8$"	5.4m	17' $8^5/_8$"
2.4m	7' $10^1/_2$"	5.7m	18' $8^3/_8$"
2.7m	8' $10^1/_4$"	5.7m	18' $8^3/_8$"
3.0m	9' $10^1/_8$"	5.7m	18' $8^3/_8$"
3.3m	10' $9^7/_8$"	6.0m	19' $8^1/_4$"
3.6m	11' $9^3/_4$"	6.3m	20' 8"
3.9m	12' $9^1/_2$"	6.6m	21' $7^7/_8$"
4.2m	13' $9^3/_8$"	6.9m	22' $7^5/_8$"
4.5m	14' $9^1/_3$"	7.2m	23' $7^1/_2$"
4.8m	15' 9"	7.5m	24' $7^1/_4$"
		7.8m	25' $7^1/_8$"

Lumber

Sizes: Metric cross-sections are so close to their nearest Imperial sizes, as noted below, that for most purposes they may be considered equivalents.

Lengths: Metric lengths are based on a 300mm module, which is slightly shorter in length than an Imperial foot. It will, therefore, be important to check your requirements accurately to the nearest inch and consult the table below to find the metric length required.

Areas: The metric area is a square meter. Use the following conversion factors when converting from Imperial data: 100 sq. feet=9,290 sq. meters.

Metric Sizes Shown Before Nearest Imperial Equivalent

millimeters	inches	millimeters	inches	millimeters	inches
16 x 75	5/8 x 3	38 x 75	$1^1/_2$ x 3	75 x 100	3 x 4
16 x 100	5/8 x 4	38 x 100	$1^1/_2$ x 4	75 x 125	3 x 5
16 x 125	5/8 x 5	38 x 125	$1^1/_2$ x 5	75 x 150	3 x 6
16 x 150	5/8 x 6	38 x 150	$1^1/_2$ x 6	75 x 175	3 x 7
19 x 75	3/4 x 3	38 x 175	$1^1/_2$ x 7	75 x 200	3 x 8
19 x 100	3/4 x 4	38 x 200	$1^1/_2$ x 8	75 x 225	3 x 9
19 x 125	3/4 x 5	38 x 225	$1^1/_2$ x 9	75 x 250	3 x 10
19 x 150	3/4 x 6	44 x 75	$1^3/_4$ x 3	75 x 300	3 x 12
22 x 75	7/8 x 3	44 x 100	$1^3/_4$ x 4	100 x 100	4 x 4
22 x 100	7/8 x 4	44 x 125	$1^3/_4$ x 5	100 x 150	4 x 6
22 x 125	7/8 x 5	44 x 150	$1^3/_4$ x 6	100 x 200	4 x 8
22 x 150	7/8 x 6	44 x 175	$1^3/_4$ x 7	100 x 250	4 x 10
25 x 75	1 x 3	44 x 200	$1^3/_4$ x 8	100 x 300	4 x 12
25 x 100	1 x 4	44 x 225	$1^3/_4$ x 9	150 x 150	6 x 6
25 x 125	1 x 5	44 x 250	$1^3/_4$ x 10	150 x 200	6 x 8
25 x 150	1 x 6	44 x 300	$1^3/_4$ x 12	150 x 300	6 x 12
25 x 175	1 x 7	50 x 75	2 x 3	200 x 200	8 x 8
25 x 200	1 x 8	50 x 100	2 x 4	250 x 250	10 x 10
25 x 225	1 x 9	50 x 125	2 x 5	300 x 300	12 x 12
25 x 250	1 x 10	50 x 150	2 x 6		
25 x 300	1 x 12	50 x 175	2 x 7		
32 x 75	$1^1/_4$ x 3	50 x 200	2 x 8		
32 x 100	$1^1/_4$ x 4	50 x 225	2 x 9		
32 x 125	$1^1/_4$ x 5	50 x 250	2 x 10		
32 x 150	$1^1/_4$ x 6	50 x 300	2 x 12		
32 x 175	$1^1/_4$ x 7	63 x 100	$2^1/_2$ x 4		
32 x 200	$1^1/_4$ x 8	63 x 125	$2^1/_2$ x 5		
32 x 225	$1^1/_4$ x 9	63 x 150	$2^1/_2$ x 6		
32 x 250	$1^1/_4$ x 10	63 x 175	$2^1/_2$ x 7		
32 x 300	$1^1/_4$ x 12	63 x 200	$2^1/_2$ x 8		
		63 x 225	$2^1/_2$ x 9		